Santa Clara University

Santa Clara, California

Written by Al Schwartz

Edited by Adam Burns and Alyson Pope

Layout by Kimberly Moore

*Additional contributions by Omid Gohari,
Christina Koshzow, Chris Mason, Joey Rahimi,
and Luke Skurman*

ISBN # 1-4274-0125-X
ISSN # 1551-0196
© Copyright 2006 College Prowler
All Rights Reserved
Printed in the U.S.A.
www.collegeprowler.com

Last Updated: 05/08/06

Special Thanks To: Babs Carryer, Andy Hannah, LaunchCyte, Tim O'Brien, Bob Sehlinger, Thomas Emerson, Andrew Skurman, Barbara Skurman, Bert Mann, Dave Lehman, Daniel Fayock, Chris Babyak, The Donald H. Jones Center for Entrepreneurship, Terry Slease, Jerry McGinnis, Bill Ecenberger, Idie McGinty, Kyle Russell, Jacque Zaremba, Larry Winderbaum, Roland Allen, Jon Reider, Team Evankovich, Lauren Varacalli, Abu Noaman, Mark Exler, Daniel Steinmeyer, Jared Cohon, Gabriela Oates, David Koegler, Glen Meakem, and the Santa Clara University Bounce-Back Team.

College Prowler®
5001 Baum Blvd.
Suite 750
Pittsburgh, PA 15213

Phone: 1-800-290-2682
Fax: 1-800-772-4972
E-Mail: info@collegeprowler.com
Web Site: www.collegeprowler.com

Welcome to College Prowler®

During the writing of College Prowler's guidebooks, we felt it was critical that our content was unbiased and unaffiliated with any college or university. We think it's important that our readers get honest information and a realistic impression of the student opinions on any campus—that's why if any aspect of a particular school is terrible, we (unlike a campus brochure) intend to publish it. While we do keep an eye out for the occasional extremist—the cheerleader or the cynic—we take pride in letting the students tell it like it is. We strive to create a book that's as representative as possible of each particular campus. Our books cover both the good and the bad, and whether the survey responses point to recurring trends or a variation in opinion, these sentiments are directly and proportionally expressed through our guides.

College Prowler guidebooks are in the hands of students throughout the entire process of their creation. Because you can't make student-written guides without the students, we have students at each campus who help write, randomly survey their peers, edit, layout, and perform accuracy checks on every book that we publish. From the very beginning, student writers gather the most up-to-date stats, facts, and inside information on their colleges. They fill each section with student quotes and summarize the findings in editorial reviews. In addition, each school receives a collection of letter grades (A through F) that reflect student opinion and help to represent contentment, prominence, or satisfaction for each of our 20 specific categories. Just as in grade school, the higher the mark the more content, more prominent, or more satisfied the students are with the particular category.

Once a book is written, additional students serve as editors and check for accuracy even more extensively. Our bounce-back team—a group of randomly selected students who have no involvement with the project—are asked to read over the material in order to help ensure that the book accurately expresses every aspect of the university and its students. This same process is applied to the 200-plus schools College Prowler currently covers. Each book is the result of endless student contributions, hundreds of pages of research and writing, and countless hours of hard work. All of this has led to the creation of a student information network that stretches across the nation to every school that we cover. It's no easy accomplishment, but it's the reason that our guides are such a great resource.

When reading our books and looking at our grades, keep in mind that every college is different and that the students who make up each school are not uniform—as a result, it is important to assess schools on a case-by-case basis. Because it's impossible to summarize an entire school with a single number or description, each book provides a dialogue, not a decision, that's made up of 20 different topics and hundreds of student quotes. In the end, we hope that this guide will serve as a valuable tool in your college selection process. Enjoy!

OMID GOHARI ○ CHRISTINA KOSHZOW ○ CHRIS MASON ○ JOEY RAHIMI ○ LUKE SKURMAN ○
The College Prowler Team

Table of Contents

Introduction from the Author

Before you continue on with this guidebook, there is one thing you need to know about Santa Clara—it is a small school. The size of the school affects everything about it, in both positive and negative ways. On the plus side, it greatly benefits students academically. It also results in a close-knit and friendly student community. The flip-side, however, is that the University has a very low national profile. I had never heard of it before my high school counselor suggested that I apply. Its teams are not on ESPN (or ESPN2, or FSN) very often. It will probably never be listed in *Playboy*'s Top Party Schools, and if that is what you want from a school, SCU is not for you. You should still buy the book, though; I could use the royalties.

Santa Clara is a unique school ("unique" sounds better than "unusual"). It's a small Jesuit university in the south Bay Area. It lacks some things that people usually associate with colleges. For example, over the last few years, I've gotten used to having this conversation—

Well-Meaning Acquaintance: "So where are you going to school again?"
Me: "Santa Clara University."
WMA: (nods and pauses) "Where is that?"
Me: "Northern California. It's in San Jose."
WMA: "Oh, nice. You like San Jose?"
Me: "Actually, I don't go into the city very much. Sometimes I go up to San Francisco; it's really close."
WMA: "How's your football team?"
Me: "Well, we don't really have a football team."
WMA: "Oh. You in a fraternity?"
Me: "No. We don't really have fraternities. Well, sort of, but they're not big. It's weird."
WMA: "Oh. (Hesitantly) So do you like it?"
Me: "Oh yeah."

To listen to myself describe the school and the surrounding area, it sounds like a drag. So why do I like it? There are several reasons. The fact that it is small, that I know almost all of my professors personally and have made friends in class, is one appealing aspect of SCU. I also like that the student body is open and accepting. The campus is beautiful, well maintained, and safe. And while I'm not crazy about the area in the immediate vicinity of campus, I enjoy the opportunities I have because of the location. On any given weekend I can go to a concert in LA, skiing in Tahoe, gambling in Reno, surfing in Santa Cruz, camping in the mountains, or bar hopping in San Francisco, and be back in time for class Monday morning. So I think SCU was the right choice for me. The question is, is it right for you? Hopefully the rest of this book can help you decide.

Al Schwartz
Author, Sanata Clara University

By the Numbers

General Information

Santa Clara University
500 El Camino Real
Santa Clara, CA 95053

Control:
Private

Academic Calendar:
Quarter (trimester)

Religious Affiliation:
Catholic (Jesuit)

Founded:
1851

Web Site:
www.scu.edu

Main Phone:
(408) 554-4000

Admissions Phone:
(408) 554-4700

Student Body

**Full-Time
Undergraduates:**
4,316

**Part-Time
Undergraduates:**
118

**Total Male
Undergraduates:**
1,940

**Total Female
Undergraduates:**
2,464

Admissions

Overall Acceptance Rate:
57%

Early Action Acceptance Rate:
75%

Regular Acceptance Rate:
54%

Total Applicants:
7,649

Total Acceptances:
4,388

Freshman Enrollment:
1,172

Yield (% of admitted students who actually enroll):
46%

Early Decision Available?
No

Early Action Available?
Yes

Early Action Deadline:
November 1

Early Action Notification:
End of December

Regular Decision Deadline:
January 15

Regular Decision Notification:
First week of April

Must-Reply-By Date:
May 1

Applicants Placed on Waiting List:
1,382

Applicants Accepted from Waiting List:
356

Students Enrolled from Waiting List:
151

Transfer Applications Received:
652

Transfer Applications Accepted:
401

Transfer Students Enrolled:
243

Transfer Application Acceptance Rate:
62%

Common Application Accepted?
Yes

Supplemental Forms?
Yes

Admissions Web Site:
www.scu.edu/ugrad

SAT I or ACT Required?
Either or both

First-Year Students Submitting SAT Scores:
96%

➜

**SAT I Range
(25th–75th Percentile):**
1110–1300

**SAT I Verbal Range
(25th–75th Percentile):**
550–640

**SAT I Math Range
(25th–75th Percentile):**
560–660

**SAT II Requirements for
Admissions:**
SAT II not required

Retention Rate:
92%

**Top 10% of High
School Class:**
37%

Application Fee:
$55

Financial Information

Tuition:
$28,899

Room and Board:
$10,032

Books and Supplies:
$1,260

**Average Need-Based
Financial Aid Package
(including loans, work-study,
grants, and other sources):**
$18,070

**Student Who Applied for
Financial Aid:**
80%

Student Who Received Aid:
52%

Financial Aid Forms:
February 1

Financial Aid Phone:
(408) 554-4505

Financial Aid E-Mail:
*www.scu.edu/financialaid/
contactus.cfm*

Financial Aid Web Site:
www.scu.edu/financialaid

Academics

The Lowdown On...
Academics

Degrees Awarded:
Bachelor
Post-Bachelor Certificate
Master
Post-Master Certificate
Doctorate

Most Popular Majors:
31% Business and Marketing
15% Social Sciences
12% Engineering
 8% Communications
 8% Psychology

Undergraduate Schools:
Arts and Sciences
Business
Counseling Psychology
Education
Engineering
Pastoral Ministries

→

Full-Time Faculty:
423

Average Course Load:
Four

Faculty with Terminal Degree:
92%

Graduation Rates:
Four-Year: 76%
Five-Year: 83%
Six-Year: 83%

Student-to-Faculty Ratio:
12:1

Special Degree Options
Work study, double major, honor's program, internships, independent study, teaching certification, study abroad programs

AP Test Score Requirements
Credit and/or placement for scores of 4 or 5

IB Test Score Requirements
Used for credit and/or placement

Best Places to Study
Library, Benson Center

Sample Academic Clubs
English Club, Pre-Health Club, Political Science Student Association

Did You Know?

For the **15th consecutive year**, SCU has been ranked second among all master's universities in the West.

The average class size at SCU is **25 students**. About 90 percent of classes have less than 50 students.

Santa Clara is on **the quarter system**, with most students skipping the summer session. The average student takes 11 or 12 classes every year, in three different sets.

What are units? Santa Clara assigns "unit" values instead of "credits" to each of its courses in order to represent the amount of work that is required by a particular class. Most lower-division classes are four units; most upper-division and lab courses are five.

Every class is taught by a professor. There are **no classes taught by TAs** at SCU.

The Leavey School of Business was ranked as the third best undergraduate business program in California.

Students Speak Out On...
Academics

"People say the workload at Santa Clara is just as hard as at Harvard or other Ivy League schools, and that it's just getting in that's harder. I don't know if that's true, but SC is definitely a tough school."

"In general, I've made it a rule to avoid Jesuit teachers. They seem a little more judgmental and less open minded than the other professors. I also try to avoid the overly feminist teachers, as they tend to be more critical of male students. All in all, however, the teachers are great; with such small classes **you get a lot of personal attention** from them."

"The **classes are really small, which is good**, but sometimes I wish they were bigger so the teacher wouldn't notice every time I skip class."

"Overall, the professors are good, but I've had one really, really bad one. I guess I should have known better than to take a class about the Bible from a Jesuit professor. I've had **some really good Jesuit teachers** in other subjects, though, so maybe it was just the one guy."

"I don't like the quarter system. I don't know why they can't make the schedule closer to the way other schools are. It also **kind of sucks to have to take three sets of finals** every year."

"**Classes are not easy**, but if you are having trouble, go to the teacher's office hours and stuff. They will help you out a lot, and showing them you're serious about it always helps."

Q "The teachers at Santa Clara take a special interest in making sure that students are engaged with the subject matter. Most will take the time to sit down personally with a student and address any confusions or concerns the student might have, or even just discuss a particular concept in more depth. **Classes are structured to encourage participation and dialogue** between peers, making them far more interesting and beneficial."

Q "Most of the teachers I have had are really good, and **they always have plenty of time to meet with you**."

Q "If it weren't for the great academics, I would say that **Santa Clara University is more like a summer resort** than a university."

The College Prowler Take On...
Academics

This is an area where Santa Clara really excels. The student/teacher ratio is one of the best in the nation, and the classes are small. If you think (as I did as a freshman) recruiting offices over-emphasize the importance of class size and student/teacher ratio, I can tell you right now they don't. It really does make a difference when you know your professor, and more importantly, he or she knows you. Classes are more intimate and productive, especially those in the arts and humanities. Also, each course is taught by an SCU professor, not a teaching assistant, so every class is led by someone knowledgeable and experienced.

The quality of a Santa Clara education is very high. It's not an easy school by any means, but you won't be working hard for nothing. The school may not get much name recognition in the Midwest or East, or from the general public of ESPN viewers, but it carries a good deal of clout among graduate schools and employers (especially on the West Coast).

The College Prowler® Grade on
Academics: B

A high Academics grade generally indicates that professors are knowledgeable, accessible, and genuinely interested in their students' welfare. Other determining factors include class size, how well professors communicate, and whether or not classes are engaging.

Local Atmosphere

The Lowdown On...
Local Atmosphere

Region:
Northern California

City, State:
Santa Clara, CA

Setting:
Urban (San Jose)

Distance from San Francisco:
45 minutes

Distance from Los Angeles:
5–7 hours
(depending on traffic)

Points of Interest:
Monterey Bay Aquarium
Pier 39
Tech Museum of Innovation
Various wineries
Winchester Mystery House
Yosemite National Park

➔

Closest Shopping Malls or Plazas:

Santana Row

Valley Fair

Closest Movie Theaters:

AMC Mercado
3111 Mission College Blvd.
Santa Clara, CA 95054
(408) 871-2AMC

AMC Saratoga 14
700 El Paseo De Saratoga
San Jose, CA 95130
(408) 871-2AMC

Major Sports Teams:

Oakland Athletics (baseball)

Oakland Raiders (football)

San Francisco 49ers (football)

San Francisco Giants (baseball)

San Jose Sharks (hockey)

City Web Sites

www.sanjoseca.gov

www.sanjose.org

Did You Know?

5 Fun Facts about San Jose:

- **San Jose** is the oldest civil settlement in California, founded in 1777.
- San Jose is **the third largest city** on the West Coast and one of the safest big cities in the nation.
- San Jose gets **300 days of sun a year**, and the average temperature is 70 degrees. Hard to beat that!
- San Jose is **the epicenter of Silicon Valley**, the technological capital of America.
- Options abound for the outdoorsy type; beaches, mountains, forests, and wine country can all be found **within 50 miles** of the city.

Famous Locals:

Fatty Arbuckle (comedian)

Neal Cassidy (Beat writer)

Brandi Chastain (soccer player)

Cesar Chavez (labor leader)

The Doobie Brothers (musicians)

Jim MacMahon (quarterback, Chicago Bears)

Stevie Nicks (musician, Fleetwood Mac)

Steve Wozniak (co-founder, Apple Computer, Inc.)

Students Speak Out On...
Local Atmosphere

"The campus is somewhat isolated, but there are lots of cool places to go to not far away, like San Francisco, Santa Cruz, and parts of San Jose."

Q "Santa Clara is a **small town shared by residents and students**. Weekends and Wednesdays seem to be happening times, but the action tends to be brought to a close rather early compared to many universities, thanks to the 'curfew conscious' SCPD."

Q "El Camino Real is a disgusting assault on the eyes. It's not like it's run-down, or an industrial area or anything. It's not Detroit ugly. It's this weird kind of California ugly, where everything is light-colored and kinda Spanish-looking, but nothing really goes together, and it seems like a constant stream of Chinese restaurants, liquor stores, and porn shops. Not that I have a problem with Chinese food, booze, or porn. But **El Camino is really ugly**."

Q "The town is friendly, but **it can be boring**. San Francisco is not too far, though."

Q "**There's a lot of outdoor stuff to do**—hiking, camping, surfing. But if you don't have a car, you're limited to campus and San Fran on the Caltrain."

Q "The campus and right around it are cool, but then **there is a big dead zone**. If you're leaving the immediate area, you have to pretty much go all the way out of San Jose to do anything cool."

Q "Santa Clara is definitely not a college town or activity center, but there are many interesting things to do and see within driving distance. **There are tons of bars, restaurants, and music in San Fran**. If you like the outdoors, there's camping in Big Sur, skiing and snowboarding in Tahoe, and the beach in Santa Cruz."

Q "Santa Clara is not the most exciting city. I spend the majority of my time within a mile radius of the University, where **there are a lot of student houses and apartments**. Anything beyond that is not that interesting, unless you are making the drive to Santa Cruz or San Francisco."

Q "It's a good place to be. **Sometimes I get bored**, but I can always go to San Francisco or Santa Cruz or something."

Although most enjoy the campus itself, many students are unimpressed with the city of Santa Clara, and to some extent, San Jose. Aside from the student housing next to campus, the nearby neighborhoods are not geared toward young people. Many students feel that the nightlife suffers because of the lack of bars and clubs near campus that usually exist at larger universities. It also does not help that El Camino Real, the "main" street in the area, is widely considered one of the ugliest streets in the country.

However, as the definition of "local" becomes broader, the opinions brighten. They may not be crazy about Santa Clara as a city, but they like it as a part of the Bay Area. There are many interesting places nearby (San Francisco, Santa Cruz, Berkeley, Monterey) to appeal to both the urban and outdoorsy types. The students seem to appreciate the options that the location affords them.

The College Prowler® Grade on
Local Atmosphere: C+

A high Local Atmosphere grade indicates that the area surrounding campus is safe and scenic. Other factors include nearby attractions, proximity to other schools, and the town's attitude toward students.

Safety & Security

The Lowdown On...
Safety & Security

Number of Campus Safety Officers:
15

Phone:
(408) 554-4441

Safety Services:
24/7 campus patrols and escort services

Emergency phones on campus

(RAD) Rape defense classes

Health Services:
Basic medical services

Counseling and psychological services

HIV testing

On-site pharmaceuticals

Health Center Office Hours:
Monday–Friday 8:30 a.m.–5 p.m.; closed during summer, but not other undergraduate breaks.

Did You Know?

Santa Clara is **one of the safest campuses** in the nation, and San Jose was once named Safest Big City in America for three years in a row (Morgan Quinto Press).

Students Speak Out On...
Safety & Security

{ **"Santa Clara is a secure campus, although there seems to be little need to bring in authorities—a majority of conflicts can be resolved civilly between participating parties."**

Q "**The campus is totally safe** as far as I'm concerned. The only thing I ever worried about was being hassled by Campus Safety when I was a freshman."

Q "There's virtually no crime, and **there're emergency phones every tenth of a mile**. The worst thing that will happen is you might have to fight with a hobo who wants your cans."

Q "**I was robbed once**, but it was by my roommate."

Q "The **only thing you have to fear on campus is Campus Safety**."

Q "You couldn't get hurt on campus if you tried. **If you got a paper cut, Campus Safety would show up** and carry you to the hospital, and there'd be a write-up about it in the *Santa Clara* (student paper)."

Q "**You'll be fine as long as you're not an idiot**. If you leave your bike or laptop laying around, it might get stolen, but that's kind of your own fault."

Q "It's never really occurred to me that campus might be dangerous. **Campus Safety is so strict**, and the police station is so close, that it's hard to imagine anything really crazy happening."

Q "For such a big city, it's very safe. **You hear the occasional rumor about roofies and date-rape** or something, but that's about it."

The College Prowler Take On...
Safety & Security

Simply put, the campus is safe. In past years, for example, serious crime on campus was limited to a half dozen cases of assault and one non-forcible sex offense. That is remarkably little crime for even a small college. The SCPD is very well funded, well staffed, and located directly across the street, so if there was an emergency, a swift response is pretty much guaranteed.

There are emergency phones all over campus, and Campus Safety is always patrolling the grounds; some students even think that the campus is a bit too safe (more on this in the Campus Strictness section). The only crime that happens with any regularity on campus is petty theft. As long as you lock your bike up and don't leave your laptop lying around unattended, you should be fine.

A

The College Prowler® Grade on

Safety & Security: A

A high grade in Safety & Security means that students generally feel safe, campus police are visible, blue-light phones and escort services are readily available, and safety precautions are not overly necessary.

Computers

The Lowdown On...
Computers

High-Speed Network?
Yes

Number of Computers:
583

Wireless Network?
Yes

Operating Systems:
Windows

Number of Labs:
2 (plus one for graduate students)

Free Software
None

Charge to Print?
Yes, each student has a SmartPrint account, with $15 a quarter. Additional money can be added to the account through a kiosk outside the computer lab in the Orradre Library.

Students Speak Out On...
Computers

> "The network could be better, but it's not too bad. You don't need a computer, but I would suggest to bring one."

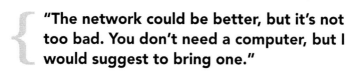 "**You don't need your own computer** here, but it's nice to have one."

Q "Students without computers can always find one on campus to use, although **during exam times there is more demand for lab space**. If nothing else, having one's own computer would guarantee some personal working space. Finished work can always be sent to yourself through e-mail and printed on campus, but new students should know that the lab computers are not equipped to make use of floppy discs, and have trouble opening documents that are not written in Word."

Q "My only complaint is that **SmartPrint should give you way more pages**."

Q "I brought my own computer, which I use mostly for porno and eBay purchases. If I'm going to do work, I'll go to the computer lab, which is **uncrowded unless it's the last week of the quarter**."

Q "You should definitely bring your own computer. I found it a good way to keep touch with some friends back home, although it's sometimes hard to get any productive work done in my room. **Laptops are too fragile, but they are nice to have, because there is wireless Internet** access in a lot of the buildings here."

Q "**File-sharing has died down a bit** since people started getting prosecuted, but students can still trade programs, songs, movies, and stuff. If both people are on the campus network, it goes really, really fast."

Q "**Most of the buildings now have wireless Internet**, so having a laptop with wireless capabilities is ideal. You can always use the computer labs if you need to."

Q "I think it's important to have a computer, but **the school's are really reliable**. I still use them sometimes."

The College Prowler Take On...
Computers

The computer network on campus is sufficient for all student needs. If you have your own computer, there are direct Ethernet connections in all the dorm rooms, and wireless networks in several buildings. Connections are fast, and the University e-mail service is reliable. Various departments also have lots of online resources. Students can use the SCU Web site to send and receive e-mail, enroll or drop classes, apply for jobs, access classroom materials, and more.

The computer labs in the library and Kenna Hall generally run pretty smoothly. They do get a bit crowded at the end of the quarter when final papers and projects are due, but even then it's rare that an open computer cannot be found in one or the other. Some students have voiced annoyance that the computers in the labs do not have disk drives, but for the most part, they seem to adapt to the new technologies quickly.

B-

The College Prowler® Grade on

Computers: B-

A high grade in Computers designates that computer labs are available, the computer network is easily accessible, and the campus's computing technology is up-to-date.

Facilities

The Lowdown On...
Facilities

Student Center:
Benson Center

Athletic Center:
Malley Center

Libraries:
2

Campus Size:
104 acres

Popular Places to Chill:
The Bronco
Cafeteria dining room
Graham Commons

What Is There to Do on Campus?

You can go for a swim, play tennis, work out on one of the dozens of exercise machines in the gym, pump iron in the weight room, surf the 'Net in the computer labs, attend mass in the historic Mission Church, have a drink or see a student band in the Bronco campus bar, do some highly marked-up grocery shopping in the Benson Center, hang out at the Multicultural Center, or catch a play or comedian in the Mayer Theater or a game in our stadium or basketball arena—all on campus. And, if you wanted to, I suppose you could study in the Orradre Library.

Movie Theater on Campus?

No

Bowling on Campus?

No

Bar on Campus?

Yes. The Bronco stages student-organized events, has a big-screen TV, pool and Ping-Pong tables, and offers beer, wine, soda, and all kinds of junk food available for late-night snacking.

Coffeehouse on Campus?

There is a coffee stand outside of the cafeteria that also serves various sandwiches, fruits, drinks, and specials. There is also Jump Start, a Jamba Juice-type juice bar behind the library.

Students Speak Out On...
Facilities

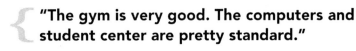

> **"The gym is very good. The computers and student center are pretty standard."**

Q "The facilities are nice on campus. **They have a good gym and a good field**, but without a football team it doesn't matter that much."

Q "**The cafeteria is pretty good**. It's a really small campus, but it has pretty much everything you would need."

Q "**The Bronco is really nice, but it's not like a real college bar**. They card really hard, so it never gets really wild. You go there to hang out, not go out, you know?"

Q "Our stadiums are all really good. **All we need is some good sports teams to go with them**, and we'd be set."

Q "**The grounds are very well kept.** Almost too well kept, because you never see anyone actually working on them. It's spooky. Like they have this whole squad of ninja gardeners who somehow mow the lawns in complete silence at 4 a.m. or something."

Q "Malley is our gym, and it is incredibly nice. The **equipment is all state-of-the-art**; there are three basketball courts, a lap swimming pool, and a workout area; a well-kept secret is the saunas in the bathrooms."

Q "The school really goes all out to make sure all the facilities are top-notch. That goes for the landscaping, too. **The dorms are pretty plain**, though. I mean, they're not bad or anything, but since they spend so much time and money improving the gym and library and stuff, you'd think the dorms would be really nice, too. But I guess they added on to Sobrato and Casa, so that's a start."

Q "**There used to be a bowling alley downstairs in Benson**, but they took it out a few years ago. I don't know why; it would be pretty sweet to be able to bowl on campus."

The College Prowler Take On...
Facilities

SCU spends huge amounts of money each year to maintain the grounds and facilities, and it shows. The campus is always clean and beautiful, and it seems like the facilities are constantly being upgraded. The equipment in the Malley Fitness Center is top-of-the-line, and the new pool is especially nice. A new addition to the Orradre Library has doubled its size. The computer labs have plenty of machines, and always have an IT staff member on duty. The Bronco bar is a fairly recent addition, and has a variety of brand-new TVs and gaming tables. The dorms seem to be a little behind the rest of the facilities, but the University has begun improving a few of them as well.

The sports fields and stadiums are high quality at SCU. Granted, Santa Clara won't be hosting a bowl game anytime soon, but the soccer field is well maintained, with plenty of seating for students. The basketball arena is quite large, considering the size of the school, and often hosts other events. Also, a new baseball stadium opened across the street from campus to support the growing success of SCU baseball. SCU spares no expense when it comes to facilities.

A-

The College Prowler® Grade on
Facilities: A-

A high Facilities grade indicates that the campus is aesthetically pleasing and well-maintained; facilities are state-of-the-art, and libraries are exceptional. Other determining factors include the quality of both athletic and student centers and an abundance of things to do on campus.

Campus Dining

The Lowdown On...
Campus Dining

Freshman Meal Plan Requirement?

Yes

Meal Plan Average Cost:

$1,145 per quarter (included in room and board)

Places to Grab a Bite with Your Meal Plan:

The Bronco

Food: Pizza, subs

Location: Benson Memorial Center

Hours: Tuesday–Thursday 9 p.m.–12:45 a.m., Friday–Saturday 9 p.m.–1:45 a.m.

Cellar Market

Food: Deli meats, produce, snacks

Location: Benson Memorial Center, lower level

Hours: Sunday–Thursday 11 a.m.–12 a.m., Friday–Saturday 11 p.m.–8 p.m.

Jump Start Café

Food: Healthy sandwiches, wraps, salads, coffee

Location: Benson Memorial Center, lower level

Hours: Monday–Friday 7:45 a.m.–6 p.m., Saturday–Sunday 12 p.m.–6 p.m.

Market Square

Food: Made-to-order, vegetarian, Italian, home-style, Latin, grill, deli

Location: Benson Memorial Center

Hours: Monday–Thursday 7 a.m.–7:30 p.m., Friday 7 a.m.–7 p.m., Saturday 10:30 a.m.–7 p.m., Sunday 10:30 a.m.–7:30 p.m.

Mission Bakery

Food: Gourmet bistro

Location: Benson Memorial Center

Hours: Monday 7 a.m.–12:30 a.m., Tuesday–Friday 7 a.m.–9:30 p.m., Saturday 8 a.m.–9:30 p.m., Sunday 8 a.m.–12:30 a.m.

Off-Campus Places to Use Your Flex Account:

Café Tandoor

Charlie Blair's Restaurant

Cramer's Bagels

DiCicco's Ristorante Italiano

Hatcho Japanese Cuisine

Henry's World Famous Hi-Life

Joy Cup

Mio Vicino

Mission City Coffee Roasting Co.

Mondo Burrito

Neto's

Quizno's

Round Table Pizza

Sara's Kitchen

Stuft Pizza

Thai Pepper

Togo's

University Chicken

Wilson's Bakery

Yum Yum Tree

Other Places that Accept Flex Accounts:

Copy Craft

Millenium Hair Salon

Rose Garden Auto Care

Salon 2001

Student Favorites:

Mondo Burrito

Sara's Kitchen

Mission City Coffee Co.

(See Off-Campus Dining for listings.)

24-Hour On-Campus Eating?

No

Flex Account

In addition to the standard Resident Meal Plan, students (or parents) can put money into a Santa Clara Flex Account. If a student has Flex money, he or she can use their Access (Student ID) Card to pay for food at any of the places listed above and at a variety of restaurants and fast food places. Flex money can also be used to print from campus computers, buy snacks from vending machines, or to buy books, supplies, and clothes at the book store.

Did You Know?

The Benson Center cafeteria offers dishes for **vegetarian and vegan students** every day.

Students Speak Out On...
Campus Dining

"Relatively speaking, the quality is good, but it's way overpriced, and there's nothing you can do about it."

Q "**It's good for cafeteria food**. But that doesn't mean it's good."

Q "Benson's good for a while, but then you start noticing things, like the **BBQ sauce, salsa, and tomato sauce on the pasta are all the same except for one ingredient**. Or the sesame chicken and rice on Thursday looks an awful lot like the Mongolian leftovers from Wednesday."

Q "**Benson memorial is good for the first two months**, until you have had everything on their menu three times over. Then it is time to venture out on your own. There are some good non-fast food restaurants."

Q "The food on campus is overall of a high quality, but it is **becoming more and more expensive each year**. There is a main dining hall where most freshmen and sophomores eat because they have dining plans. However, for those that live off campus, there are many more price conscious options. There is also a market that sells many nonperishable items and frozen goods. There is an emphasis on junk food, but there are some more health conscious options. A place similar to Jamba Juice, which makes food to go, smoothies, and coffee, is also on campus. It is popular, but expensive. The service we get for the food we pay for is good."

Q "Bon Appetite provides a quality product that tends to go unappreciated until students move off campus and realize they don't have easy access to it anymore. However, there are a **wide variety of restaurants that students can use their Flex money** at, which is convenient and satisfactory."

Q "Benson overall is not bad. **It gets a bad rap because you have to eat it every day**, but as far as college food goes, it's pretty good. There is a lot of variety each day, although one bad burrito and you may never go back."

Q "**Bronco food is a late-night guilty pleasure**. It's all terrible for you, but it's nice to take a break from studying and chow down on greasy pizza and chicken strips or a big sundae sometimes."

Q "I stop by the Mission Bakery stand on my way to class every morning to grab a bagel and some orange juice or coffee. **It's not bad, and it's very convenient**."

The College Prowler Take On...
Campus Dining

All students living on campus (this means you, freshmen) receive a dining plan as part—a rather large part—of their housing costs. Every quarter, the student receives dining points that can be used to buy food in the cafeteria, the Bronco, the Cellar Market, and a few other places. This is a lot more than most students who eat two meals a day on campus will need, even though the food is high priced. The catch is that at the end of the quarter, you can only carry over or be refunded about $60 of that money. So often times students will go on Cellar market shopping sprees at the end of the quarter to spend the extra money. They may not even really want some of the stuff, but since they're not getting the money back anyway, what the hell?

Quality-wise, the food is much better than most college cafeterias. There are several stations (a burger grill, an Italian station, a vegetarian station) that each have a permanent menu and lunch and dinner specials every day. This provides a much better variety than most cafeterias offer, but to regular diners, the specials will start looking familiar fairly quickly. The Bronco, which is open much later than the cafeteria, also serves food, mainly of the pizza, nacho, and fried varieties—not as healthy, but essential for any student from time to time.

B

The College Prowler® Grade on

Campus Dining: B

Our grade on Campus Dining addresses the quality of both school-owned dining halls and independent on-campus restaurants as well as the price, availability, and variety of food.

Off-Campus Dining

The Lowdown On...
Off-Campus Dining

Restaurant Prowler:
Popular Places to Eat!

Charlie Blair's Restaurant
Food: Italian
940 Monroe St.
(408) 423-9045
Price: $6–$10 per person
Hours: Monday–Thursday
11 a.m.–9 p.m.,
Friday 11 a.m.–10 p.m.,
Saturday 12 p.m.–10 p.m.

Fast Delivery Pizza
Food: Pizza
341 Lafayette St. Ste. 104
(408) 246-1800
Price: $4–$8 per person
Hours: Daily 11 a.m.–11 p.m.

→

Henry's World Famous Hi-Life

Food: Barbeque

301 W Saint John St.

(408) 295-5414

www.henryshilife.com

Price: $15–$20 per person

Hours: Monday 5 p.m.–
9 p.m., Tuesday–Thursday
11:30 a.m.–2 p.m., 5 p.m.–
9 p.m., Friday 11:30 a.m.–
2 p.m., 5 p.m.–9:30 p.m.,
Saturday 4 p.m.–9:30 p.m.,
Sunday 4 p.m.–9 p.m.

Mio Vicino

Food: Italian

1290 Benton St.

(408) 241-9414

Cool Features: Private dining
room available, premium
wine list

Price: $10–$15 per person

Hours: Monday–Friday
11:30 a.m.–10 p.m.,
Saturday–Sunday 5 p.m.–
10 p.m.

Mission City Coffee Roasting Co.

Food: Coffee, bakery

2221 The Alameda

(408) 261-2221

Cool Features: Wireless
Internet

Price: $2–$8 per person

Hours: Daily 7 a.m.–11 p.m.

Mondo Burrito

Food: Mexican

3300 The Alameda

(408) 260-9596

Cool Features: Fresh, healthy
ingredients, outdoor dining

Price: $4–$6 per person

Hours: Monday–Friday
11 a.m.–9 p.m.,
Saturday 11:30 a.m.–8 p.m.

Mr. Chau's Chinese

Food: Chinese

2165 El Camino Real

(408) 261-2298

Price: $5–$7 per person

Hours: Daily 11 a.m.–9 p.m.

Sara's Kitchen

Food: American

1595 Franklin St.

(408) 247-7272

Cool Features: Great
breakfast

Price: $6–$10 per person

Hours: Tuesday–Friday
7 a.m.–2:30 p.m., 4:30 p.m.–
8 p.m., Saturday–Sunday
7 a.m.–3 p.m.

Stuft Pizza

Food: Pizza

2898 Homestead Rd.

(408) 244-9444

Price: $6–$8 per person

Hours: Sunday–Thursday
11 a.m.–9:30 p.m., Friday–
Saturday 11 a.m.–10 p.m.

Subway

Food: Subs, salads

1171 Homestead Rd.

(408) 247-2191

Price: $6–$8 per person

Hours: Monday–Friday 9 a.m.–8 p.m., Saturday–Sunday 9 a.m.–6 p.m.

Thai Pepper

Food: Thai

1045 Monroe St.

(408) 984-1931

Price: $6–$10 per person

Hours: Daily 11 a.m.–3 p.m., 5 p.m.–10 p.m.

University Chicken (Cluck-U Chicken)

Food: Chicken

2562 The Alameda

(408) 241-2582

Cool Features: 911 Challenge—some of the hottest wings in California

Hours: Sunday–Thursday 11 a.m.–12 a.m., Friday–Saturday 11 a.m.–2 a.m.

Student Favorites

Fast Delivery Pizza, located about a block off campus has the best pizza around, whole or by the slice. Nearby fast food chains are particularly popular with students who are up late, drunk, high, short on cash, or some combination of the four.

Late-Night, Half-Price Food Specials

University Chicken, Charlie Blair's Restaurant, and Stuft Pizza all have specials for students (Senior Night, etc.) on a regular basis.

Other Places to Check Out:

Hungry Hound
In-N-Out Burger
Jack in the Box
La Victoria
Maggiano's Little Italy
McDonald's
Neto Sausage Co.
Su's Mongolian Barbeque Restaurant
Taco Bell

Closest Grocery Store:

Safeway
(actually closer to campus than one of the dorms)
2605 The Alameda
(408) 244-6873

Best Pizza:

Fast Delivery

Best Chinese:

Thai Pepper (sit-down)
Mr. Chau's (fast food)

Best Breakfast:

Sara's Kitchen

Best Wings:

University Chicken

Best Healthy:

Mission City Coffee Co.
Subway

Best Place to Take Your Parents:

Henry's World Famous Hi-Life
Thai Pepper
Mio Vicino

Many students visit nearby San Francisco or Los Gatos for dinner when their parents visit.

Students Speak Out On...
Off-Campus Dining

"Stuft Pizza, Cluck-U, Henry's, Mio Vicino, Sarah's Kitchen—all yummy."

Q "After freshman year, I was totally burned out on Benson food, and I never cook for myself. But **there are so many places to eat that I can walk to** that I get plenty of variety."

Q "**Neto's barbeque is awesome**. They grill all these different types of sausages and steaks outside, and you take yours in and make a sandwich out of it. It's my favorite place to eat by far, but they only do the BBQ on Tuesdays and Fridays for some reason. Maybe that's good, I might overdo it if I could get it every day."

Q "The best restaurants are **Henry's, Hungry Hound, Thai Pepper, and Su's Mongolian**."

Q "The restaurants around campus are good. **La Victoria is the best one for good cheap food**. Cluck U is also very good; there's nothing like convincing a drunk friend to take the 911 challenge (a super-hot, hot wing-eating test), and watching him writhe in agony after two bites."

Q "With Flex, you can tell your parents that your books were $600 when they were only $300 and **eat off the rest**, freeing up extra cash."

Q "**I lived off Fast Delivery pizza for about two months** last year. I think I could do it again."

Q "There are plenty of places to eat around here, but **one glaring problem—no White Castles**. I can't believe they don't have one within a block of every college in the country."

Q "**My parents put money on Flex**, because they think otherwise I'll spend it on drugs, booze, or gambling."

Q "Coming from out-of-state, **everyone told me how great In-N-Out Burger was**. I knew about it from *The Big Lebowski*, so I tried it out. It sucked. Do yourself a favor and don't go there."

Q "My favorite places are Mondo, but I wouldn't call that a restaurant, and Thai Pepper. Then **there is Santana Row, which has a bunch of really nice places** like Maggiano's, a great Italian place."

The College Prowler Take On...
Off-Campus Dining

There is a variety of off-campus dining within walking distance from campus. Mexican, Chinese, Italian, BBQ, bakeries, fast food; you can find just about whatever you want. The one area lacking options is upscale, sit-down restaurants. You'll have to head to San Jose or Los Gatos for that. But just because something is cheap doesn't mean it's not good. Fast Delivery Pizza, Mondo Burrito, and Mission City Bakery are all delicious and affordable.

The Flex Account is a good option for students who want to expand their dining options, or parents who may be a little worried about where the money they're spending on food or books is actually ending up. Most places within a few blocks of campus accept it, and a few that are further off. The exceptions are fast food chains like McDonald's, Jack in the Box, and Taco Bell, the absence of which may actually sweeten the deal for concerned parents.

The College Prowler® Grade on
Off-Campus
Dining: B+

A high Off-Campus Dining grade implies that off-campus restaurants are affordable, accessible, and worth visiting. Other factors include the variety of cuisine and the availability of alternative options (vegetarian, vegan, Kosher, etc.).

Campus Housing

The Lowdown On...
Campus Housing

Undergrads Living on Campus:
48%

Best Dorms:
Casa Italiana
Graham Complex

Worst Dorms:
North Alameda
Swig*

*Swig has a reputation for being the "party dorm," and therefore being a bit loud and dirty. So the reasons for its inclusion on the "Worst" list may actually appeal to some.

Dormitories:

Alameda North
Floors: 2
Total Occupancy: 69
Bathrooms: In-room
Coed: Yes
Residents: Freshmen, sophomores, juniors, seniors
Room Types: Doubles
Special Features: TV lounge, laundry, study area, swimming pool, private parking

Campisi
Floors: 3
Total Occupancy: 190
Bathrooms: Shared by floor
Coed: Yes
Residents: Freshmen, sophomores, juniors, seniors
Room Types: Doubles
Special Features: In-room sinks, TV lounge, study room, kitchen

Casa Italiana
Floors: 4
Total Occupancy: 299
Bathrooms: In-room
Coed: Yes
Residents: Freshmen, sophomores, juniors, seniors
Room Types: Singles, suites, apartments
Special Features: Classrooms, seminar rooms, faculty and staff offices

Dunne
Floors: 5
Total Occupancy: 271
Bathroom: Shared by floor
Coed: Yes
Residents: Freshmen, sophomores, juniors, seniors
Room Types: Double
Special Features: TV lounge, vending machines, laundry

Graham Complex
Floors: 2 (four buildings)
Total Occupancy: 240
Bathrooms: Shared by floor
Coed: Yes
Residents: Freshmen, sophomores, juniors, seniors
Room Types: Doubles
Special Features: Garden and barbeque area, TV lounge, vending machines, laundry

McLaughlin
Floors: 3
Total Occupancy: 121
Bathroom: Shared by floor
Coed: Yes
Residents: Freshmen, sophomores, juniors, seniors
Room Types: Doubles
Special Features: In-room sinks, TV lounge, study lounge, vending machines, laundry

San Fillipo

Floors: 3

Total Occupancy: 194

Bathrooms: Shared by floor

Coed: Yes

Residents: Freshmen, sophomores, juniors, seniors

Room Types: Doubles

Special Features: TV lounge, kitchen, laundry facilities, study rooms

Sobrato

Floors: 4

Total Occupancy: 277

Bathrooms: In-room

Coed: Yes

Residents: Freshmen, sophomores, juniors, seniors

Room Types: Singles, suites, apartments

Special Features: Laundry, classrooms, seminar rooms, faculty and staff offices

Swig

Floors: 10

Total Occupancy: 345

Bathrooms: Shared by floor

Coed: Yes

Residents: Freshmen, sophomores, juniors, seniors

Room Types: Double

Special Features: In-room sinks, TV lounges, study lounges, vending machines

Walsh

Floors: 3

Total Occupancy: 90

Bathrooms: Shared by floor

Coed: Yes

Residents: Freshmen, sophomores, juniors, seniors

Room Types: Double

Special Features: TV lounges, study lounges, vending machines, laundry, kitchen

Housing Offered:

Singles: 10%

Doubles: 66%

Triples/Suites: 13%

Apartments: 11%

Room Types

Most of the freshman dorms are pretty much the same. There are two dorms that have nicer, suite-style rooms, but one is reserved for upperclassmen (Sobrato), and the other is for students in the Italian studies program (Casa Italiana). Freshman dorms consist mostly of two-person rooms, with a few larger triple rooms.

Bed Type

Twin extra-long (39"x80"); lofts and bunk-beds available

Available for Rent

Alhambra water coolers and water delivery

Cleaning Service?

In public areas; community and semi-private bathrooms are cleaned by staff approximately once a week.

You Get

Bed, desk and chair, bookshelf, dresser, closet or wardrobe, window coverings, cable TV jack, Ethernet or wireless Internet connection, free campus and local phone calls

Smoke-Free Dorms

All buildings are smoke-free, and smoking is prohibited within 25 feet of dormitories.

Did You Know?

All campus residents get **free cable** and access to SCU's movie channel, as well as the campus Ethernet/wireless network.

Students Speak Out On...
Campus Housing

> "Not one of the dorms is terrible. There are several newer ones that tend to be in high demand—Sobrato and Casa. But it's more about the people you're living with than where you're living."

Q "**The dorms are very plain**. Stay away from Swig. There are a bunch of savages in that place."

Q "**RLCs weren't that helpful**, but it was nice to have classes with people in my dorm first quarter."

Q "**They spend so much money on landscaping** and flowers and stuff, but I would rather have AC in the dorms, or toilet paper that's soft and effective."

Q "The rooms are like any other dorm rooms. **It's nice that they all have Ethernet connections**, though."

Q "Freshman year, **the RA on my floor wrote up a bunch of people for drinking**. Then one night he got wasted and passed out on the toilet; pants down and everything. So we called Campus Safety and told them we thought he had alcohol poisoning. There's some great video footage of them waking him up. Huh? What does that have to do with on-campus housing? Well, it happened in a dorm. Duh."

Q "**Avoid Swig unless you like paying a lot of fines for puke in the elevator and bathrooms**. Graham was nice when they had the pool, but that is gone now, so I guess Campisi and San Filipo would be best."

Q "**They got rid of the Graham pool for some reason**, which sucks. The actual pool was small and nothing special, but it was a cool place to hang out. And the freshman girls lying out by it were always nice."

Q "I liked living in the dorms, but I was ready to move off campus after the first year. **Campus Safety and the RAs are just too strict**. Sometimes it felt like they were trying to baby-sit me. Then other times I felt like they were trying to get me arrested. Like when they called the Santa Clara Police to come arrest me. I didn't like that."

The College Prowler Take On...
Campus Housing

The dorm rooms at SCU are just that—dorm rooms. They are not particularly large or small, and they come with minimal furnishings. The underclassman dorms are pretty much interchangeable, with the exception of Swig and Alameda North. Swig is considered the worst dorm because of its reputation rather than any problems with the facilities; it is really very similar to the others. Alameda North is a bit different because of its location on the "Dark Side" of campus (thus called because of its distance from the center of campus) and is a converted apartment building. The rooms are setup a little differently, and it is more isolated than the other dorms. It is the preferred dorm for sophomores who wanted to move off campus but were unable to for one reason or another.

The biggest complaint students have about the dorms is the strictness. While this varies to some degree depending on the RA, they are all fairly strict. Campus Safety will check into any noise or activity they think is suspicious, and sometimes search the rooms of students they catch breaking the rules, even if they were not in their room at the time of the infraction. This is more of an annoyance than anything, though, because if you get in trouble every week or get caught with drugs, punishments are usually light. All in all, the dorms are average but a little strict.

B-

The College Prowler® Grade on

Campus Housing: B-

A high Campus Housing grade indicates that dorms are clean, well-maintained, and spacious. Other determining factors include variety of dorms, proximity to classes, and social atmosphere.

Off-Campus Housing

The Lowdown On...
Off-Campus Housing

Undergrads in Off-Campus Housing:
52%

Average Rent for:
Studio Apt.: $450/month
1BR Apt.: $500/month
2BR Apt.: $800/month

Best Time to Look for a Place:
End of winter/beginning of spring quarter

For Assistance Contact:
Office of Student Life
www.scu.edu/studentlife/housing/index
(408) 554-4583
jrosenberger@scu.edu

Students Speak Out On...
Off-Campus Housing

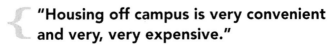

"Housing off campus is very convenient and very, very expensive."

Q "**It's all monopolized by Real Source**, but you gotta do it. The whole social scene is based around student house parties. Besides, who wants to live in the dorms for four years?"

Q "**There's this guy who goes around student houses in the morning and takes all their empty cans for recycling** or something. He scared the hell out of me the first time I saw him, since I had no idea who the weirdo in our backyard was. But now I figure if you want the stuff, go nuts. It's not like I'm doing anything with it."

Q "It's a good setup. We have a nice house that's one of the farthest away from campus, but it's still, like, **a four-minute walk to class**."

Q "**The prices are ridiculously high**, but I think it is better living off campus by a long shot. I like being able to have parties at my house and not having to worry about Campus Safety."

Q "I'd say more than half of sophomores stay on campus, but **almost all juniors and seniors move off**. Housing is outrageously expensive; individual rent often runs between $500 to $600 a month for a shared room in a run-down college house. Apartments are a little more affordable, but houses are a lot more fun because you can host parties."

Q "**Finding off-campus housing can be a hassle**. You need to start looking early, like winter quarter of the year before you're moving in. If you don't, all the houses near campus will be taken, and you'll have to take an apartment or a house farther away."

Q "There is this **one crazy lady in the neighborhood who always videotapes the students partying** and walking around to show to the police. It's definitely weird, but I guess the cops don't pay any attention to her, so everybody pretty much ignores her."

Q "The rules are strict on campus. Here, **I make the rules**. Here, I am God!"

The College Prowler Take On...
Off-Campus Housing

Most students move into off-campus housing sophomore or junior year, because the social scene revolves around off-campus student houses and apartments. Property costs in the area are very high, and year-round leases are often required even though the students will only be there for 8 to 9 months of it. This is especially true of properties that are very close to campus. However, since the student body on the whole is fairly wealthy, and since living on campus is not exactly cheap anyway, price is usually not a deal breaker.

I advise students to consider moving off campus. The price difference is usually worth it for the extra freedom and comfort having a place of one's own provides, and convenience is pretty much a non-issue. (When I first moved off campus, my walks to class were actually shorter than the previous year.) Those interested in moving off campus should start looking during winter quarter. That is when leases for the fall start becoming available for houses whose residents are graduating, moving, or just can't get organized enough to commit to another year. The Office of Student Life has an online directory of available off-campus housing at *www.scu.edu/studentlife/housing*.

B

The College Prowler® Grade on

**Off-Campus
Housing: B**

A high Campus Housing grade indicates that dorms are clean, well-maintained, and spacious. Other determining factors include variety of dorms, proximity to classes, and social atmosphere.

Diversity

The Lowdown On...
Diversity

Native American:
1%

White:
60%

Asian American:
19%

International:
4%

African American:
3%

Out-of-State:
32%

Hispanic:
13%

Political Activity

Most students are politically and socially liberal, but not uniformly so. The religious history of the school and its location in the Bay Area contribute to a fairly diverse political climate. Rallies and protests on or near campus are infrequent. Many politically-active students are members of the Santa Clara Community Action Program (SCCAP).

Gay Pride

The gay community at Santa Clara is relatively small and accepted by almost all. Any hostility one might fear because of the school's religious affiliation is either unfounded or outweighed by the fact that the school is in the Bay Area, one of the most liberal areas of the country, and was founded by Jesuits, who are among the most liberal Catholics.

Most Popular Religions

A majority of the student body is Christian, with Roman Catholic being the most common denomination. Almost 25 percent of the student body defines itself as "unaffiliated" religiously.

Economic Status

While by no means made up entirely of "rich kids," much of the student body seems to come from fairly wealthy backgrounds (as tends to happen when it costs upwards of $38,000 a year to attend a school).

Minority Clubs

Arab Cultural Society, Asian-Pacific Islander Student Union, Black Student Union, Chinese Student Union, Filipino Student Union, Hawaiian Student Union, Intandesh (South Asian), Latino Student Union, Vietnamese Student Union

Students Speak Out On...
Diversity

> "Santa Clara does not cultivate interracial mingling. For that matter, it doesn't seem to cultivate relations between the wealthy and non-wealthy. Rich people tend to be pretty exclusive about their company."

Q "Santa Clara tries to provide outlets for minorities, like the Unity living situation and various ethnic clubs. Racial groups remain very segregated and a bit clique-ish. There are rumors of token ethnic persons being paid to appear at Greek functions to avoid trouble with the chapter. Fraternities and sororities, other than those specifically set aside for minority groups, are white, white, and more white. Just take a look at the photos on their walls."

Q "There were some gay dudes hooking up on our hammock last week. I never had that happen in Kansas."

Q "It's diverse, but clique-y. All the Hawaiians and Asians hang out, and there's the Latino frat. Only the hippies really intermix a lot."

Q "Racially, it's pretty diverse. Culturally, not so much."

Q "I hear the Multicultural Center is really cool, but since I'm white, I feel like I wouldn't be very welcome. So I've never actually been inside it."

Q "There are a ton of whites, a lot of Asians and Hispanics, quite a few Arabs, and almost no blacks. That's not terribly diverse, I guess, but **it's not like _School Ties_ or anything**. Most people come from such similar backgrounds that race is not such a big deal."

Q "I think right around half the student body is some kind of minority. A lot of those are Asian, though, and 60 percent white isn't that diverse anyway. It's not really a big issue, though. I guess **it's moderately diverse, but very tolerant**."

Q "Diversity? Yeah right, **diversity at Santa Clara ranges from white to albino**. Except the engineering school, where they have some Asians, too."

The College Prowler Take On...
Diversity

This seems like a good place to address SCU's religious status. There are many Jesuits on the faculty, including the president of the University, and there is a large Catholic community. If you are Catholic, that's great. But if you aren't, or come from a Catholic school background but are not religious (like me), the school's religious affiliation may make you more reluctant to enroll. Don't worry about it. You won't be forced to go to mass or do something Christian around holidays. Among the several Jesuit professors I've had here, none have started preaching in class or been forceful about their beliefs. So if you were hesitating because of that, don't sweat it.

That being said, Santa Clara is not the most diverse school out there. Whites and Roman Catholics make up the bulk of the student body. This is not to say that there is no diversity, but certain demographics are largely unrepresented. For example, there are sizable numbers of Hispanic and Asian American students, but very few African Americans; many non-Catholic students, but few practicing non-Christians. However, the area where SC is most homogenous is not race or religion, but economic background. Sure, there are some students on full scholarship who do not have a lot of money, but for the most part, the student body ranges from slightly rich to Uncle-Scrooge-from-*Duck-Tales* rich.

The College Prowler® Grade on
Diversity: C+

A high grade in Diversity indicates that ethnic minorities and international students have a notable presence on campus and that students of different economic backgrounds, religious beliefs, and sexual preferences are well-represented.

Guys & Girls

The Lowdown On...
Guys & Girls

Men Undergrads:	Women Undergrads:
43%	57%

Birth Control Available?
No

Most Prevalent STDs on Campus
Chlamydia

Social Scene

This is a big concern for most incoming freshmen. It helps that all the dorms are coed, and the RLC system makes it likely that you will live near many of the people you have class with. If you want to meet a variety of people at the beginning of the year, you can always join a bunch of clubs you have no intention of actively participating in. The social scene is based on house parties, which are usually non-exclusive except for some frat parties.

Best Place to Meet Guys/Girls

House parties, fraternities and sororities, classes, athletic events

Did You Know?

Top Three Places to Find Hotties:

1. The pool
2. Volleyball court
3. Athletic events

Top Places to Hook Up:

1. Library basement
2. 11th floor, Swig Hall
3. House parties
4. RA's room (although successes are difficult to verify, the attempt is considered mandatory to many students)
5. Gym sauna

Dress Code

Styles vary on campus, but they can be generally classified according to certain groups.

Male Styles – Major. Fun Fact about Wearer. (Footwear):

Frattastic – Business/Marketing. An ugly girl threw up in his mouth at a house party freshman year. (Doc Martens)

Casual – English. Took first test of collegiate career still drunk from the preceding Tuesday night—failed. (New Balance)

Hippie – Religious Studies. Drove 2006 Jeep Liberty to Berkeley to protest nation's dependence on foreign oil. (No shoes)

Female Styles – Sample Top/Bottom. What it Says about Her. (Peak Season*):

Party Girl – Tank top/miniskirt with neon red thong visible. I'm three cups of jungle juice away from puking in a Sig Pi's mouth. (Fall)

Wallflower – Sweatshirt/jeans. The Freshman 15 is NOT a myth. (Winter)

Girl Next Door – Tight sweater/tight jeans. I'm more intelligent than that lush in the thong. What a slut. (Spring)

*Note – It is possible for a single student to employ two or even all three styles, sometimes in a single year.

Students Speak Out On...
Guys & Girls

> "Most of the guys are cool. From my experience, the hot girls are often snobby, stupid, and rich, but there are exceptions."

Q "The Santa Clara population offers little in the way of males. There seems to be a **high school mentality among both sexes**, but this is particularly noticeable in the fraternity-oriented groups. Guys seem to know how to dress nice, but not how to take care of themselves."

Q "Girls are on the attractive side, but there is **far too much emphasis placed on looking good**. I wouldn't be surprised to find out many girls spend more time on their outfits and makeup than they do on their studies. There's a lot of pressure to maintain a hot body, and guys and girls spend a lot of their free time in the gym."

Q "I, personally, am **very attractive**."

Q "I've been seeing way **too many of those wannabe Abercrombie & Fitch** merts with their polo collars popped. It's obvious they spent a lot of time trying to make it look like they didn't spend any time on their look. The girls are pretty hot; a lot of them are kinda stuck-up, though. But there are some that are really cool."

Q "There is a perception that **nobody here really dates**. It's kind of true; at least I can't think of very many people with significant others."

Q "**The social scene here isn't conducive to meeting people and hooking up**. You're options (socially) are pretty limited, so you tend to see the same people all the time."

Q "One thing that surprises me, since we're such as small school, is **how little mingling there is with non-Santa Clara students**. Sometimes people from San Jose State come around, but not that much. So if you look at your classmates and don't like what you see, tough luck. That's what you have to work with."

Q "SCU is **almost 60 percent female**. You gotta like those odds."

The College Prowler Take On...
Guys & Girls

While the student body is, on average, rather attractive, some students seem pessimistic about this category. Most of their complaints are actually about the nightlife or Greek system. They feel that the social scene is not conducive enough to hooking up, which may be true to some extent. Combined with the small size of the school and the RLC system that groups students together in both classes and the dorms, one's options can seem narrower than they really are. The social scene is rather limited, but it is also open enough that meeting new people is not at all difficult if you try. It also helps to explore many fronts—parties, of course, but also clubs, athletic events, and classes. Since the student body is around 60 percent female, the guys have slightly wider options than the girls.

Pledging with a fraternity or sorority freshman year ensures that you will have plenty of opportunities to interact with drunk members of the opposite sex, but since they will mostly be other Greeks, it can have a limiting effect on your selection as well. Also, the benefits of going Greek drop off once everyone settles into their own niche, so think about it before you decide. Whatever you decide, keep in mind that Santa Clara is not a huge party school, so random hookups are not as common as they are at some schools. That being said, it is college, so of course they happen.

The College Prowler® Grade on
Guys: B

A high grade for Guys indicates that the male population on campus is attractive, smart, friendly, and engaging, and that the school has a decent ratio of guys to girls.

The College Prowler® Grade on
Girls: B+

A high grade for Girls not only implies that the women on campus are attractive, smart, friendly, and engaging, but also that there is a fair ratio of girls to guys.

Athletics

The Lowdown On...
Athletics

Athletic Division:
NCAA Division I

Conference:
West Coast Conference

School Mascot:
Bronco

**Men Playing
Varsity Sports:**
155 (8%)

**Women Playing
Varsity Sports:**
142 (6%)

➜

Men's Varsity Sports:

Baseball
Basketball
Crew
Cross-Country
Golf
Soccer
Tennis
Water Polo

Women's Varsity Sports:

Basketball
Crew
Cross-Country
Golf
Soccer
Tennis
Volleyball
Water Polo

Club Sports:

Boxing (Men's)
Lacrosse (Men's, Women's)
Rugby (Men's, Women's)
Volleyball (Men's)

Intramurals:

Badminton
Basketball
Flag Football
Kickball
Soccer
Softball
Table Tennis
Tennis
Ultimate Frisbee
Volleyball

Athletic Fields

Buck Shaw Stadium, Intramural Field, Stephen Schott
Baseball Stadium

Getting Tickets

Tickets to sporting events are easy to come by. The only time
it may be necessary to buy tickets in advance is when we play
men's basketball rival Gonzaga.

Most Popular Sports

Basketball and baseball are the most popular men's sports. Women's soccer has been growing in popularity and success in recent years.

Overlooked Teams

The men's water polo team has been improving recently. Club boxing has also been growing in popularity among the student body.

Best Place to Take a Walk

San Jose Municipal Rose Garden

Gyms/Facilities

Pat Malley Fitness Center

Opened in 1999, the Malley Center features a variety of well-maintained fitness equipment, including treadmills, stationary bikes, rowing machines, Stairmasters, and various weight training machines, as well as basketball courts and a swimming pool.

Outdoor Tennis Courts

These six beautiful outdoor courts are built into the ground and lit for nighttime play.

Students Speak Out On...
Athletics

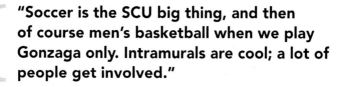

"Soccer is the SCU big thing, and then of course men's basketball when we play Gonzaga only. Intramurals are cool; a lot of people get involved."

Q "Athletics seems to attract minimal attention compared to other universities. Though our teams are good and the athletes extremely devoted, there always seems to be a **considerable lack of supporters present**, even at home games. Maybe because scheduled games are not widely publicized."

Q "Intramural sports are pretty huge, especially flag football, basketball, and soccer. If we were better at basketball and actually had a football team, varsity sports would be a lot better. We do have a good soccer program; it's always **fun to watch the girls on ESPN playing for a national title**."

Q "Varsity sports are not very big. **There's no football team, and thus no real school spirit**."

Q "No football team. Our basketball team sucks. All we have is soccer, and that's not really big. Well, it's bigger than at a lot of schools, probably, but **beggars can't be choosers**."

Q "Sports are not that big on campus, since there is no football and the basketball team isn't very good. **It's a lot of fun when we play Gonzaga**, but most of the time you don't even notice the lack of spirit."

Q "**I started going to boxing matches** when my friend joined the team. It's fun to get wasted and watch a bunch of dudes pounding each other."

Q "I don't know why more people don't go to sporting events. **Our teams are really good for our size**, and it's really cheap if you join the Ruff Riders (student booster group). I guess not having a football team discourages some people right off the bat. And there are always some who just think it's cool to be blasé about everything."

The College Prowler Take On...
Athletics

Varsity sports are not a huge part of Santa Clara life. The most notable example is the lack of a varsity football team. This means no tailgating, no Homecoming, no Bowl games, and less school spirit. And although it is a Division I school, SCU's small size makes it hard for the school to be competitive in many major sports. This is not to say that SCU sports are weak or ignored. Both the men's and women's soccer teams are contenders for the national title every year, and women's volleyball has placed very high in the nation for the last several years. Baseball is also growing in success and popularity, and the basketball arena is always packed when the men play division rival Gonzaga. Almost half the student body joins the student booster group, the Ruff Riders.

Recreational sports are very popular on campus. It seems like everyone is on one intramural team or another. Flag football games are common sights in the fall, and winter basketball leagues can get especially competitive. There are also men's, women's, and coed soccer and softball leagues throughout the year, and who in their right mind would pass up a chance to play competitive kickball? It seems that the lack of "serious" varsity programs allows the students to have a lot of fun with sports.

The College Prowler® Grade on

Athletics: B-

A high grade in Athletics indicates that students have school spirit, that sports programs are respected, that games are well-attended, and that intramurals are a prominent part of student life.

Nightlife

The Lowdown On...
Nightlife

Club and Bar Prowler:
Popular Nightlife Spots!

Club Crawler:
While clubbing is not very popular among SCU students, it is not due to a lack of places to go. The newly renovated Santana Row, about one mile from campus, has several nightclubs to choose from, but the hottest spots, like Toons and Zoe, are located in downtown San Jose.

Toons Nightclub

52 E Santa Clara St.

(408) 292-7464

Toon's is popular with students for its dance floor with live music and DJs. If you need a break from dancing, there is a back room with pool tables, pinball machines, video games, darts, and air hockey. There is no cover if you have a student ID.

Zoe Bar & Grill Nightclub

417 S 1st St.

(408) 971-6647

Zoe's caters to the hip hop crowd and offers several dance areas. This club occasionally hosts famous rap artists like 2 Live Crew.

Bar Prowler:

The Hut, located directly across the street from campus, is the most popular bar in the area, frequently offering student specials (like Senior Night). Blinky's Can't Say Lounge offers a more low-key atmosphere. C&J's has live entertainment semi-regularly, but is less popular because it is farther off campus and is a little more expensive.

Blinky's Can't Say Lounge

1031 Franklin Sq.

(408) 985-7201

This sports bar is decortated with game photos and autographs from famous sports stars from the Bay area.

C&J's Sports Bar

1550 Lafayette St.

(408) 423-9013

C&J's is very casual, perfect for a night of relaxing, meeting up with friends, and sharing drinks. There is live music and several TVs.

Claran Cocktail Lounge

1251 Franklin Sq.

(408) 248-4682

Claran's is a '60s-style lounge that has been recently renovated. There is a dance floor and games like pool, darts, arcade games, and TVs.

The Hut

3200 The Alameda

(408) 920-2597

www.thehutsantaclara.com

The Hut is a Santa Clara staple. Students flock here for the drink specials and weekend DJs. The Hut also has a pool table and TVs.

Bars Close At:

2 a.m.

Primary Areas with Nightlife:

Downtown San Jose

San Francisco

Santana Row

Cheapest Place to Get a Drink:

Blinky's Can't Say Lounge

Student Favorites:

The Hut

Useful Resources for Nightlife:

www.sanjose.com/nightlife

www.clubvibes.com/index.asp?city=48

Wave magazine

The Santa Clara student paper

Favorite Drinking Games:

Beer Pong

Card Games (Kings, Circle of Death, F*** the Dealer)

Century Club

Power Hour

What to Do if You're Not 21

The Bronco bar in the Benson Center is open to students of all ages, and student bands play there almost every week.

House Parties

House parties are the basis of the SCU social scene. The neighborhood on the southwest side of campus is comprised mostly of student houses, condos, and apartments, and on any weekend night (and often Wednesdays and Thursdays), there are multiple parties going on. With the exception of some of the stricter fraternity parties, pretty much everyone is welcome at any of them.

Frats

See the Greek section!

Students Speak Out On...
Nightlife

{ **"Parties on campus? Haha, nonexistent, unless you call illegally drinking in your dorm room a party. There are clubs in San Jose, if that's your thing, but the majority of 21 year olds go to local bars."**

Q "**The Hut is the main student bar**; it isn't bad, but it isn't good; Better then the other places around here. The owners are cool. There are usually three big parties a year, one by each fraternity. I am in a fraternity, so I think those parties are the best, of course. Plus, we have mixers with sororities, and those are a blast; usually better than open parties."

Q "**Parties get old quickly and are quite repetitive**. They are usually broken up before things have time to really get going, leaving clumps of students wandering the streets drunk and aimless. That's when it's nice to have a house of your own, so you and your friends have somewhere to fall back on."

Q "Legal drinkers tend to pack into one campus-affiliated bar, the Hut. When it's busy, the outside section is the place to be, but ordering and paying can be frustrating. The bar lacks sufficient entertainment, other than a pool table that is too crowded to play on. For live music and other sorts of entertainment, **the Bronco is far more promising and open**."

Q "The Santa Clara police have too much money and officers for the amount of actual crime that goes on. It's not unusual to see three brand-new cop cars, one of them an SUV, show up to break up a party and write a forty-eight. **It sucks when they break up all the big parties early in the night**."

Q "The parties can be fun if they don't get broken up early. Some houses have more problems with the cops, probably due to location. **Your average keg party will usually get warned by the cops at about 11 p.m.** and die down for 45 minutes or an hour, and then everyone will get drunk and loud again and it will get busted for real at one or two in the morning."

Q **"If you came to Santa Clara for the nightlife, I don't know what you were thinking**. There is one main bar, which is alright, but not great. There are no clubs around, just keg parties, and they usually get broken up around midnight."

The College Prowler Take On...
Nightlife

Many students are disappointed with the nightlife at Santa Clara. There are only a few bars within walking distance of campus, and no clubs. So few that if someone tells you they are "going to the bar," you can be 90 percent sure that they are referring to the Hut. Dance clubs are not popular among the students, at least partly because they are not convenient. To do any real clubbing you'll have to head into San Jose, which probably means springing for a taxi.

The lack of bars and clubs near campus means that house parties dominate the social scene. The good news is that they are numerous and cheaper than going to a bar. For the most part, they are also receptive to almost everyone and safe. The SCPD breaks them up frequently, but usually just gives warnings to the owners of the house. Partygoers themselves are hardly ever ticketed. The bad news is that they are house parties. That means lots of people in small spaces, long waits to get a foamy cup of Natural Light, and even longer ones to use the bathroom. If that kind of party is not your cup of tea (or Natty, as it were), you will need to find some like-minded people to go out with, and one of you better have a car.

The College Prowler® Grade on
Nightlife: C-

A high grade in Nightlife indicates that there are many bars and clubs in the area that are easily accessible and affordable. Other determining factors include the number of options for the under-21 crowd and the prevalence of house parties.

Greek Life

The Lowdown On...
Greek Life

Number of Fraternities:

2.5*

*California Phi is not an official fraternity, but functions almost exactly like the others.

Number of Sororities:

3

Undergrad Men inFraternities:

7%

Undergrad Women in Sororities:

5%

→

Fraternities on Campus:

Sigma Pi

Pi Kappa Alpha (Pike)

California Phi

Sororities on Campus:

Alpha Phi

Kappa Alpha Theta (Theta)

Delta Gamma (DG)

Multicultural Colonies:

Nu Alpha Kappa

Did You Know?

The Greek system at SCU is unique. Several years ago, **the University stopped acknowledging Greek organizations**, which were never very large or numerous, saying that they conflicted with the school's Jesuit values. At about the same time, the SAE fraternity house had its charter revoked by its national council for hazing infractions. The Greek system still survives in an unsanctioned form, even the SAE house, which became California Phi.

Students Speak Out On...
Greek Life

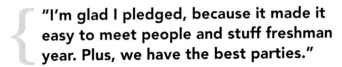

> **"I'm glad I pledged, because it made it easy to meet people and stuff freshman year. Plus, we have the best parties."**

Q "If you are looking for a way to meet people and have the need to be a part of something, I'd recommend Greek life. If you are able to make a good group of friends without a formal organization, then I wouldn't do it. It doesn't dominate the social scene, and **becomes less and less important after your freshman year**."

Q "The Greek life at SC is **very pretentious and exclusive**. Screw it."

Q "The Greek system at a school with a large population can be cool. This school **doesn't have a large population**, so . . ."

Q "Most of the big parties are organized by the fraternities, which are not associated with the school. **Greek life here is pathetic compared to bigger schools like USC or UCLA**. We only have two fraternities you hear about, and then a fraternity turned "social club" because they lost their charter. Sorority choices are slim as well, only three. Fraternity life does make social life a lot better, though. As a member of a fraternity, we have events every week like going to ball games, going bowling, drinking activity nights, playing sports, and other stuff. It allows for a more interesting time because you can always find someone who wants to do what you want to do."

Q "The frats are not great, but Cal Phi really sucks. It isn't even a frat; **it's just a house that you can pay to be friends with**."

Q "For a while, freshman year, I wished I had joined a frat because they had parties and stuff to do, while the rest of us wandered around on the streets. But after I settled in, **I was glad I didn't pledge**, because those benefits didn't seem as important, and some of the frat guys really suck."

Q "Day parties on Saturday afternoons at the frats are **some of the best times of the year**. For some reason people seem to get a lot drunker during the day. It's a good chance to go all out and party like a rock star, especially if you live on campus most of the time."

The College Prowler Take On...
Greek Life

Greek life at Santa Clara is unique and complicated, but to put it simply, it's not a very big deal. Since the Greek system is not recognized by the school, they are not allowed to organize, or even advertise, events on campus. Also, the fraternity and sorority houses are much smaller than those at larger schools. This affects them in several ways. First, only a handful of members actually live in the house (although there are a few non-official houses where members of a certain frat traditionally live). Second, frat parties are not huge events like at bigger schools. They are generally better organized, slightly larger versions of the house parties that go on every week.

There are benefits to the low visibility of the SCU Greek system as well. Pledging a fraternity or sorority is not such a dominant force in a student's life as it would be elsewhere. Hazing is not a problem, and it is normal for a pledge to have a fairly extensive network of friends who are not affiliated with their house. Pledging is also a good way to meet people freshman year, especially members of the opposite sex, so if you are having trouble finding your niche at first, considering going Greek might be a good idea.

The College Prowler® Grade on
Greek Life: D

A high grade in Greek Life indicates that sororities and fraternities are not only present, but also active on campus. Other determining factors include the variety of houses available and the respect the Greek community receives from the rest of the campus.

Drug Scene

The Lowdown On...
Drug Scene

Most Prevalent Drugs on Campus:

Adderall

Alcohol

Marijuana

Liquor-Related Referals:

683

Liquor-Related Arrests:

80

Drug-Related Referals:

95

Drug-Related Arrests:

16

Drug Counseling Programs

SCU offers a variety of substance abuse programs all free-of-charge for students.

Santa Clara University Counseling Center

500 El Camino Real, Benson 201

(408) 554-4172

www.scu.edu/SCU/Centers/Counseling/staff.html

Students Speak Out On...
Drug Scene

"Marijuana is a definite staple among the students, as is alcohol. Other drug use is not widely publicized. Students probably experiment with hallucinogenic drugs and barbiturates, but there does not seem to be heavy traffic of it."

Q "**Prescription drugs are in high demand**. Ritalin, Adderall, and Stratera are very popular as study aids and are passed around rather freely. Also, a large percentage of students are on mood stabilizers and are fairly open in discussing it."

Q "The cops are pretty lax. We were **smoking a bong on the Dive's (apartment) balcony** one time, and a cop came up and told us to—quote—'take our bong rips inside.'"

Q "The few **people who do drugs stick to marijuana**, which is usually chronic."

Q "**There aren't any drugs on campus**. Once you're off, they're around, of course. But I don't know anyone here who has a serious problem."

Q "Drugs aren't big here; it's not a party school. **A lot of people smoke weed, but that's about it**. One time I saw some people do some coke at a party, but you could tell most people thought it was weird, and I've never seen it happen again."

Q "Adderall is all over the place. **It's like a kind of currency on campus**. People sell it or trade it for other drugs. Most people just use it to study, but a few take it as a party drug before they go out, which I just don't get."

Q "Drugs are not all over the place or anything, but it's like everywhere—**you can find them if you look**. Well, you might have a problem if you wanted crack or something. But how many college students smoke crack anyway? And Santa Clara's a really good, hard school, so that kind of thing is even more uncommon."

Q "**Drugs are pretty popular here**. But where aren't drugs popular?"

The College Prowler Take On...
Drug Scene

The drug scene at SCU is miniscule compared to most colleges. There is some hallucinogenic use, but it's pretty covert. Every once in a while you hear about someone doing cocaine. Hard drug (heroin, crack) use is nonexistent. Prescription painkillers are somewhat common in a few circles. There is a fair amount of trafficking of study aides like Adderall and Ritalin among students, especially during finals week. However, the only drug that is prevalent around campus is marijuana.

Marijuana is widely used by SCU students. If you searched every off-campus student apartment or house, you would probably find weed or paraphernalia in most. This may be because high-quality grass is easy to come by in the area. California has experienced efforts to legalize medical marijuana, most of which have been based in the Bay Area. Because of this, much of the marijuana available comes from Cannabis Clubs or home growers, and is therefore quite potent, and considered relatively safe. Of course, you can never be completely sure what you are getting from a drug dealer. But all in all, drug use among students is neither extensive nor particularly threatening.

B-

The College Prowler® Grade on

Drug Scene: B-

A high grade in the Drug Scene indicates that drugs are not a noticeable part of campus life; drug use is not visible, and no pressure to use them seems to exist.

Campus Strictness

The Lowdown On...
Campus Strictness

What Are You Most Likely to Get Caught Doing on Campus?

- Drinking underage
- Public urination or indecency
- Parking illegally
- Making too much noise in your dorm
- Sending unsolicited e-mail (spam)
- Vandalism or theft of University property

Students Speak Out On...
Campus Strictness

"Campus Safety is way too strict about drinking and stuff. It must be a conspiracy. The Man is always trying to hold me down."

Q "They are very strict. Campus Safety, with a few exceptions, has a complex about not being real police officers, which transfers into mistreatment of students. **A lot of them have power trips**, and don't act very professionally. I get the sense that they don't respect the students and take out their frustration on us."

Q "The Campus Safety are pretty bad; **they tend to be antagonistic towards the students**."

Q "Depending on how many times you are caught and the amount of drugs you have on you, **you could be turned over to SCPD**. Drinking wise, they just make you write an essay or a poster, maybe pay a fine. Nothing big at all; they take the drugs more seriously than the drinking."

Q "They are really strict, but it's not like there's anywhere to party on campus or anything. Get in good with your RA and **don't do anything really stupid, and you shouldn't have any problems**."

Q "I know when the Bronco first opened up, **no one would even try to use a fake ID there it was so strict**. Maybe it's loosened up some since then. I don't know, it's been a while since I had to worry about that stuff."

Q "If you're underage, **you need to watch out for the ABC (plain-clothes police officers)** outside of Safeway. They usually drive vans, and will run up to the car if they see someone who looks young come out with beer. They got me like two months before I turned 21, and it was a huge ordeal."

Q "They're really strict about drinking on campus, which is kind of lame. It's college, though, so plenty of it still goes on. When you get caught, the actual **punishment usually isn't bad, but Campus Safety can be real jerks** about it when they bust you."

The College Prowler Take On...
Campus Strictness

It seems like almost everyone has a story of the time they were just minding their own business and some Campus Safety guy started harassing them. Luckily, the harassing is always of the "he made me put out my cigarette because I was too close to the building" variety instead of the "he hit me in the head with a flashlight fourteen times" kind. Everyone agrees that the campus is perfectly safe, and oftentimes point to this as evidence that Campus Safety is largely useless; they tend to overlook the part the strictness plays in keeping it that way. CS certainly can be overzealous (I have a story or two of my own), but try to keep in mind that they are providing a service for the students.

That being said, you better watch yourself. CS officers seem to take particular relish in ferreting out corruption on their beats. This usually takes the form of a bottle of tequila in a dorm room closet or backpack full of Busch Light on a freshman. If you are caught, terrible consequences await you, such as taking online alcohol awareness classes. These usually consist of starting a video on your computer and hanging out in someone else's room for half an hour. When you return, you will have to take a test on the material with questions like "What should you do if your pregnant friend is drunk and gets into a fight with her boyfriend at a party?" (Hint—don't let her drive.) Anyway, unless you get in trouble multiple times in a single quarter, it should not be too difficult to avoid being fined or arrested.

The College Prowler® Grade on

Campus
Strictness: C-

A high Campus Strictness grade implies an overall lenient atmosphere; police and RAs are fairly tolerant, and the administration's rules are flexible.

Parking

The Lowdown On...
Parking

Approximate Parking Permit Cost:

$210 per year

SCU Parking Services:

Phone: (408) 554-4441

Fax: (408) 554-7882

Student Parking Lot?

No

Freshmen Allowed to Park?

Yes

Common Parking Tickets:

Expired Time (One-Hour Parking): $30

No-Parking Zone: $40

Handicapped Zone: $200

Fire Lane: $100

Parking Permits

While a car is certainly not necessary, many students who live on campus bring them. If you plan to, a parking permit is essential. Annual, semi-annual, quarterly, and nighttime permits are offered through the Campus Safety Web site at *www.scu.edu/cs/PARKING.htm.*

Did You Know?

Best Places to Find a Parking Spot
• F-Lot (in the "L" on the south side of campus).

• Anywhere after 5 p.m. (all parking lots are open)

Good Luck Getting a Parking Spot Here!
• A-, B-, C-, D-, and E-Lots during weekdays.

Students Speak Out On...

Parking

> **"It is much easier to just make the walk than try to find parking. Really, after trying to find a spot for half an hour, you would have made it to class quicker if you just walked."**

Q "**Parking on campus is limited and expensive**. And the whole area is strictly enforced."

Q "You need a permit, which is pretty competitive to get. I **wouldn't recommend a car freshman year**."

Q "Parking is terrible. I've gotten many tickets for parking in front of my own house while I was going through the difficult process of getting a permit. **The meter maids are not very nice or forgiving**."

Q "If you leave your car in a two-hour parking zone for two hours and five minutes, **that meter maid will get you**. You can try and protest and say you'll move it, but one look into her dead, soulless eyes will convince you that you're getting off easy with a fine."

Q "Parking permits are expensive for those living on campus. For those off campus, all the streets are two- or four-hour parking, so it is hard for us to keep our car in one spot, especially since **each household is allowed only two permits**, which is ridiculous when there are up to 10 people living in a house."

Q "You definitely don't need a car for everyday use, just getting to class and stuff. But you are going to need one eventually, or you're going to go crazy from being stuck in Santa Clara. I'd recommend bringing a car if you can, but don't use it that much, and **park it way off campus**."

Q "Parking sucks. I think **they only give out a hundred freshman permits**, so you have to get lucky to get one. It helps if you have a job on campus, I think."

The College Prowler Take On...
Parking

Parking near campus can be a problem. Spaces can be difficult to find during the week, but it is not nearly as bad as in many cities. Finding a spot is only half the problem, though. Parking restrictions are enforced very strictly, so be ready to move your car frequently during restricted hours (weekdays) if you don't have a permit. Tickets are so frequent, however, that you really should buy one if you are bringing a car. Permits for freshmen can be difficult to obtain, but you'll need one, so you should contact Campus Safety as early as possible. They are fairly cheap compared to some schools. Of course, if you plan on sticking around school most of the time, you won't actually need a car. The campus is small enough that it is much more convenient for anyone living on or near campus to walk to classes than to drive.

The College Prowler® Grade on
Parking: D+

A high grade in this section indicates that parking is both available and affordable, and that parking enforcement isn't overly severe.

Transportation

The Lowdown On...
Transportation

Ways to Get Around Town:

On Campus
Skateboards, walking (it's a really small campus)

Public Transportation
Directly across El Camino Real from the main campus entrance is a city bus/airport shuttle/Caltrain stop. With some planning ahead of time, you should be able to get wherever you want to go from there.

Valley Transportation Authority
(408) 321-2300
(800) 894-9908
Buses run efficiently, although not as frequently as a visitor might like. Operators can help you plan routes.

Taxi Cabs
A1 American Cab Co.
(408) 260-1144

Alpha Cab Express Service
(408) 295-9500

➜

(Taxi Cabs, continued)

Scott Blvd.
(408) 727-2277

Los Gatos Cab
(408) 244-3131

Car Rentals

Avis
local: (408) 248-7300
national: (800) 831-2847
www.avis.com

Budget
local: (408) 979-0111
national: (800) 527-0700
www.budget.com

Dollar
local: (408) 292-9400
national: (800) 800-4000
www.dollar.com

Enterprise
local: (408) 492-0501
national: (800) 736-8222
www.enterprise.com

Hertz
local: (408) 844-9357
national: (800) 654-3131
www.hertz.com

National
local: (408) 970-0270
national: (800) 227-7368
www.nationalcar.com

Best Ways to Get Around Town

Buses, bikes, hoofing it. Find a kid on your floor with a car, and make friends with him right away.

Ways to Get Out of Town:

Airlines Serving San Jose

Alaska Airlines
(800) 426-0333
www.alaskaair.com

American Airlines
(800) 433-7300
www.americanairlines.com

Continental
(800) 523-3273
www.continental.com

Delta
(800) 221-1212
www.delta-air.com

Frontier Airlines
(800)-432-1359
www.frontierairlines.com

Horizon Airlines
(800)-547-9308
www.horizonair.com

Jet Blue
(800)-538-2583
www.jetblue.com

Mexicana
(800)-531-7921
www.mexicana.com

Northwest
(800) 225-2525
www.nwa.com

Southwest
(800) 435-9792
www.southwest.com

United
(800) 241-6522
www.united.com

Airport

San Jose International Airport, (408) 501-7600

San Jose International is practically right on top of campus. There is a shuttle that stops directly across the street from the main entrance that can get you there in about 15 minutes, but if you have your own car, you can be there in as little as five.

How to Get to the Airport

The SJC Airport Flyer shuttle makes the rounds from the Airport Terminals to the Metro Light Rail Station to the Santa Clara Caltrain station every 15 minutes. It is free. A cab ride to the airport costs around $10 or less.

Greyhound

The Greyhound Trailways Bus Terminal is in downtown San Jose, approximately three miles from campus. For schedule information, call (800) 231-2222.

www.greyhound.com

San Jose Greyhound Station
65 Cahill St.,
San Jose, CA
(408) 287-7462

Amtrak

The Amtrak Train Station is in downtown San Jose, approximately three miles from campus (same as the Greyhound station). For schedule information, call (800) 872-7245.

www.amtrak.com

San Jose Amtrak Train Station
65 Cahill St.,
San Jose, CA
(408) 287-7462

Travel Agents

M&K Travel Service

12 S 1st St. Ste. 909
San Jose, CA

(408) 955-0772

O'Brien Travel Service

42 S 1st St. Ste. E
San Jose, CA

(408) 275-6611

The Discerning Traveler
111 W Saint John St.
San Jose, CA

(408) 998-2719

Students Speak Out On...
Transportation

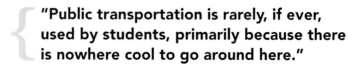

"Public transportation is rarely, if ever, used by students, primarily because there is nowhere cool to go around here."

Q "You start to **take for granted how convenient it is to be so close to the airport**. You can get there in five minutes, and the lines and security there usually move pretty fast, even on holidays. At home, I have to leave for the airport more than an hour earlier than I do here."

Q "The **Caltrain is a good, cheap way to get to San Fran** for the day. I take it to go to Giants and Niner games sometimes."

Q "The only thing I have used is **the shuttle to the airport, which is very convenient**."

Q "Everyone is so rich they probably **haven't even heard of public transportation**."

Q "**Caltrain is cheap and easy**, but they've been doing a bunch of construction on it lately. I used to use it quite a bit to go to San Fran, but I haven't in a long time."

Q "There is plenty of public transportation, but **no one ever uses it**, because if you are leaving campus, you might as well leave the whole city."

Q "We used to use Caltrain before all my friends got cars. Now **we drive everywhere**."

The College Prowler Take On...
Transportation

Transportation to and from campus is very convenient. San Jose International Airport is only a few minutes away, but you won't be kept up at night by planes taking off and landing. Shuttles run from the airport to campus non-stop, so even a total newcomer should be able to find his way between them without difficulty. The Caltrain station directly across the street from the main entrance to campus is a quick and easy way to get to San Francisco and Oakland or almost anywhere else in the Bay Area on the cheap. There is also a city bus stop there, but it is rarely utilized by students, because it only comes a few times a day.

For those who are not keen on public transportation, there are a number of taxi services available. Several major highways, including the 101, 880, and 280, also intersect within a half mile of campus, making navigating off-campus excursions fairly simple for those with cars of their own. The transportation options are such that students can make their way pretty much anywhere they want with a minimal amount of planning.

The College Prowler® Grade on
Transportation: A-

A high grade for Transportation indicates that campus buses, public buses, cabs, and rental cars are readily-available and affordable. Other determining factors include proximity to an airport and the necessity of transportation.

Weather

The Lowdown On...
Weather

Average Temperature:

Fall:	63 °F
Winter:	54 °F
Spring:	77 °F
Summer:	83 °F

Average Precipitation:

Fall:	1.54 in.
Winter:	2.85 in.
Spring:	0.52 in.
Summer:	0.12 in.

Students Speak Out On...
Weather

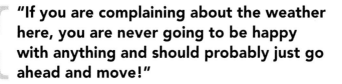

"If you are complaining about the weather here, you are never going to be happy with anything and should probably just go ahead and move!"

Q "It is pretty warm here from May to October. Really hot in the summer, sort of cold in the winter. **It can get up to a hundred**, but never drops below forty. The winters can be wet, but not even close to other places like Oregon or the East Coast."

Q "What? There isn't any weather here! Seriously, coming from the Midwest, I'm used to much more extreme weather than we ever get here. It can get kind of cold in the winter, but a sweatshirt will take care of it; **you never need gloves, a hat, earmuffs, or any of that stuff**."

Q "**It gets cold and rainy in the winter**, but the spring, summer, and fall are all just about perfect."

Q "How should I put this? **Gorgeous**! It does get a little cold in the winter. Sometimes you have to wear a sweatshirt."

Q "It's pretty cold for California. I came from down South, and **it gets hotter and colder here than I expected**."

Q "I was kind of **expecting it to be totally tropical**, which was dumb, of course. It gets a little cold, but it's completely manageable."

Q "It hardly ever rains, and it never storms. It doesn't even really get windy. So **it's pretty calm all the time**. I'm still waiting for a big earthquake to liven things up a bit."

Q "It's **funny in the winter to watch freshman girls still go out in miniskirts** and little tops and everything. They can't be at all comfortable in that stuff, but it's just barely warm enough that they will try to wear them."

The College Prowler Take On...
Weather

The weather is mostly mild and pleasant. Some students from out-of-state come expecting it to always be hot and sunny, but this is Northern California, not San Diego. Even they cannot complain much about the weather, though. It is hot in the summer, cool in the winter, and just about perfect in the spring and fall. It rains lightly, mostly in the winter, but there are no thunderstorms, snow, or other extreme weather.

Do bring some warm clothes, though, since it does get chilly in the winter, especially as you get closer to the coast or the bay. For example, San Francisco, while less than 50 miles away, is usually 10 to 15 degrees colder than San Jose. And although it never snows in the city, many students bring skiing and snowboarding gear and buy season passes to resorts in Tahoe, a few hours away. On the other hand, if you should find the mild winters too dreary, a weekend at the beach in Santa Barbara is just as simple.

The College Prowler® Grade on
Weather: A-

A high Weather grade designates that temperatures are mild and rarely reach extremes, that the campus tends to be sunny rather than rainy, and that weather is fairly consistent rather than unpredictable.

Report Card Summary

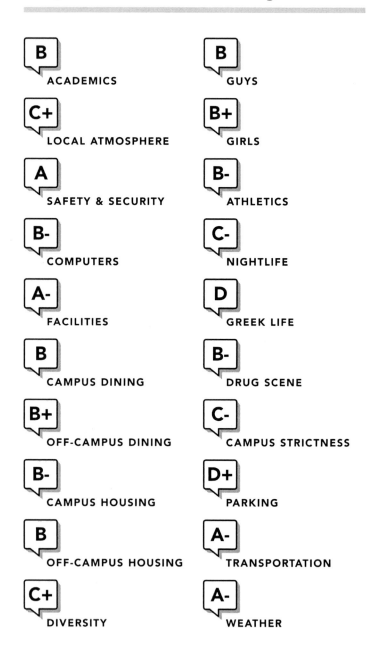

B
ACADEMICS

B
GUYS

C+
LOCAL ATMOSPHERE

B+
GIRLS

A
SAFETY & SECURITY

B-
ATHLETICS

B-
COMPUTERS

C-
NIGHTLIFE

A-
FACILITIES

D
GREEK LIFE

B
CAMPUS DINING

B-
DRUG SCENE

B+
OFF-CAMPUS DINING

C-
CAMPUS STRICTNESS

B-
CAMPUS HOUSING

D+
PARKING

B
OFF-CAMPUS HOUSING

A-
TRANSPORTATION

C+
DIVERSITY

A-
WEATHER

Overall Experience

Students Speak Out On...
Overall Experience

> "Santa Clara is an awesome school if you make the most of it. This requires some effort on your part to get involved in the many different things there are to do here. But nobody's going to make you do it, so you'll have to be motivated coming in."

"I am from pretty close, about 30 miles away. I came here to be reasonably close to my folks and still have a great education from a prestigious university that will allow me to continue my education at grad school. **I would give my experience here a 7.5 out of 10**. I would like it to be a bigger school with more of a social atmosphere, but if I was, then my grades would probably be worse than they already are, so it's probably good that I am here."

Q "**Campus is beautiful**, the surrounding area blows, small classes, bunch of loser frat guys, bunch of hot girls, no football, basketball's getting good, and facilities are good. What else? Oh, there's high-quality weed all over the place."

Q "The **desolation of the surrounding area forces the students into a tight-knit community**. I like that community, even if there are some frat guys I'm not crazy about."

Q "I like it, but it's all what you put into it. Some people get down on the school early on; you know, as soon as they get here they're saying the social life sucks and we don't have a football team or whatever. I think those **people are really missing out on all the good stuff SC has to offer**."

Q "**I wish I could go here for four more years**. Without, you know, having to pay for it, or work, or anything."

Q "The small size has benefits and drawbacks. It's a pretty tight community, but **sometimes it is too much like high school**."

Q "The **teachers give you a lot of attention** and are good about hooking you up with jobs or grad school applications after graduation."

Q "Sometimes I think that **this school and everyone in it is completely lame**. Then I see something like a couch burning in the middle of the street and think, 'Damn, somebody just got totally radical,' and it gives me hope."

The College Prowler Take On...
Overall Experience

Santa Clara is not like most schools. It is a small, Jesuit university, and its strengths and weaknesses stem from that. The academics and facilities are top-notch, and the school spares no expense on the facilities. The size of the school makes it difficult to remain competitive in Division I sports, but baseball and men's and women's soccer are always contenders, and men's basketball has begun receiving national attention in the past few years. The social scene is limited compared to larger schools, but it is also less exclusive and stressful. So should you come to Santa Clara?

It depends what you want from college. If you want a high-quality education, you should definitely come; if you want *Girls Gone Wild* to do a special at your frat house, probably not. If you like surfing, skiing, hiking, climbing, or the outdoors in general, you will like the area; if you want to go clubbing four nights a week, you probably won't. If you're into drinking or smoking pot, the scene here probably won't disappoint you; if you prefer blowing coke or dropping E, it probably will.

The Inside Scoop

The Lowdown On...
The Inside Scoop

SCU Slang:

Know the slang, know the school. The following is a list of things you really need to know before coming to SCU. The more of these words you know, the better off you'll be.

Cheefing – A practical joke involving writing on a sleeping victim with a marker.

The Dark Side – The north side of campus, where there is a small section of student housing.

Frat-tastic – Adjective describing the more enthusiastic fraternity members.

Forty-Eight – A noise violation warning, stating that if the police are called to the same house again within forty-eight hours, the occupants will be fined.

Mert – Derogatory term for someone who believes they are cool, but, in fact, are not.

RLC – Residential Learning Community. Not really very important.

Weak Sauce – Adjective describing something negative or uncool. Example: "I was at this cool party on the Dark Side, and a couple of merts started getting rowdy, so the cops came and gave us a forty-eight. It was totally weak sauce."

Things I Wish I Knew Before Coming to SCU

• RLCs don't mean that much.

• The Greek system is a lot different than other schools.

• The ABC watches Safeway all the time.

• How to surf better (the locals at Santa Cruz keep threatening my life).

• That I would need a car to go to all the cool places.

• What a "mert" is.

• They are really serious about that "Two-Hour Parking" sign.

Tips to Succeed at SCU

• Show up to class every day and participate (the professors will notice if you don't).

• Go to professors' office hours to get one-on-one help.

• Stay out of Campus Safety's way, and especially don't drink or smoke in the open.

• Don't try to take all Tuesday/Thursday classes. Sure, a four-day weekend sounds great, but by the time you go to your fourth class, your brain will no longer be processing new information.

• Take advantage of all the resources at the Career Center to find a job or internship that is right for you.

SCU Urban Legends

- Santa Clara classes are actually harder than at Ivy League schools, where good grades are (supposedly) easy to come by once you get in.

- The band Sublime played their last show in the Brass Rail, shortly before lead singer Brad Nowell overdosed on a nearby beach.

- Bon Appetite (the company who runs the cafeteria) treats their food with a chemical in order to prevent food poisoning, but the chemical triggers explosive diarrhea in certain people.

- Ten to twenty years ago, the University sold the "USC" acronym to the University of Southern California for an obscene amount of money.

School Spirit

Almost half the student body is part of the Ruff Riders booster club.

Traditions

During exam week, groups of students will often lighten the somber atmosphere by streaking through the library and Benson Center.

Midnight breakfast in the Benson Center is a significant social event for new students every fall.

Dads and Grads – The morning of graduation, students and their fathers go to the Hut bar to "prepare" for the ceremony.

At least once a year, a couch is burned in the middle of Market Street. No one seems to know exactly why.

Finding a Job or Internship

The Lowdown On...
Finding a Job or Internship

The SCU Career Center offers various services to students, including aptitude testing, resumé building assistance, and BroncoTrak, an online database of jobs and internships in the Bay Area and around the country that will hire SCU students.

Advice

Get on BroncoTRAK as soon as possible and set some criteria for the jobs you want. The database will continuously e-mail you information about new openings that match your description. It is good to get into the habit of following up on all your applications through e-mail, or preferably a phone call a few days after you submit them. Also, you need to learn to sell yourself; first in writing and then verbally. As the saying goes, "the resumé may result in an interview, but it's the interview that wins you the job." There is a whole new lexicon that you need to know for job applications. For instance, you need to use words like "lexicon," which sound impressive and professional. The Career Center can help you with all this.

Career Center Resources & Services

BroncoTRAK

Campus employment

Career counseling

Graduate school advising

Interviewing and Management workshops

Placement advising

The Resource Center

Average Salary Information

The average starting salary among MBA alumni with full-time employment at the time of graduation was $81,044.

Alumni

The Lowdown On...
Alumni

Web Site:
www.scu.edu/alumni

Office:
Santa Clara University
Alumni Association
500 El Camino Real
Santa Clara, CA 95053
(408) 554-6800
(866) 554-6800
Fax: (408) 554-2155

Services Available:
Alumni Audit Program
Alumni magazine
Awards
Career networking
MBNA alumni Mastercard
Monthly newsletter
Online community
Scholarships
Temporary medical insurance

Major Alumni Events:

Class reunions

Graduation Picnic

Homecoming

Vintage Santa Clara

Alumni Publications:

The *SC Magazine* is automatically sent to alumni free of charge, and is also available online.

Did You Know?

Famous SCU Alumni:

Andy Ackerman (Class of '78) – TV producer and director, *Seinfeld*

Edmund G. "Jerry" Brown, Jr. (Class of '59) – Mayor of Oakland, former governor of California

Brandi Chastain (Class of '91) – Professional soccer player, World Cup

Shemar Moore (Class of '93) – TV actor, *Soul Train* host

Steve Nash (Class of '96) – Professional basketball player, Phoenix Suns

Leon Panetta (Class of '60, JD '63) – Former White House chief of staff, U.S. Congressman

Student Organizations

Multicultural Center Clubs

Arab Cultural Society

Asian Pacific Islander Student Union (APSU)

Barkada (Filipino Student Association)

Chinese Student Association (CSA)

Intandesh (South Asian Student Association)

Igwebuike (Pan African Student Association)

Ka Mana'o O Hawaii

M.E.Ch.A-El Frente (Latino)

Vietnamese Student Association

Other Clubs

Accounting Association

Alpha Psi Omega (Theatre Honor's Society)

American Marketing Association

American Society of Civil Engineers

Anthropology Club

Badminton

Ballet Folklorico Los Potrillos de Santa Clara

Boxing Club

Calpulli Huitzilopochtli Aztec Dance

Car Club of SCU

Cheer

Chicanos and Latinos in Engineering and Sciences

Chicanos and Latinos in Health Education (CHE)

Cinema Club

Club Volleyball Team (Men's)

College Democrats

College Republicans

Commuter Student Body

Core Christian Fellowship

Creativity Club

Dance Team

Delta Omicron International Music Fraternity

Delta Sigma Pi (Business Society)

Dum Dum Band

Economics Club

English Club

Entrepreneur Organization

Equestrian Club

Ethnic Studies

Classical Fencing Club

Finance Association

Ultimate Frisbee

Lacrosse Team (Men's)

Lacrosse (Women's)

Le Club Francophone

Future Educators of SCU (FESCU)

Bisexual, Gay, Questioning, and Lesbian Alliance (GALA)

Gay & Straight People for Education of Diversity (GASPED)

German Club

Gospel Choir

Grassroots-Environmental Efforts Now (GREEN!)

International Club

Iranian Student Organization (ISO)

Italian Club

Jewish Student Union

Shotokan Karate Club

Kickball League

Latino Business Student Association

Management Association

Math/Computer Science Society

Model UN

Muslim Student Association

National Society of Black Engineers (NSBE)

National Society of Collegiate Scholars (NSCS)

.NET User Group

OMIS Student Network (OSN)

Pi Mu Epsilon (PME) (Math Society)

Political Science Student Association

Pre-Health Club

Psychology Club

Rock Climbing

Ruff Riders

Rugby (Women's)

Sailing

Salsa Clara

Santa Clarans Against Drunk Driving (SCADD)

Santa Clara Students for Higher Education

Scuba

SCUTS Rugby (Men's)

Serbian Students of Santa Clara

Shamrox SCU's Irish Dance Club

Sister Speaks

Society of Music

Society of Women Engineers

Society for Promotion of Arts and Mayhem (SPAM)

Sociology Student Association

Student Association for Solidarity with Salvadorans

Student Athlete Leadership Council

Students in Free Enterprise

Surfing Association

Tae Kwon Do

Tau Beta Pi (Honor's Society)

Tempura Anime

TV Club

SC Undergrads for Democracy

Vagabond Society

Volleyball (Women's)

Women's Club

Wushu (martial arts)

The Best & Worst

The Ten BEST Things About SCU

1	Personal attention from professors
2	It's close to everything
3	Safety
4	Live music at the Bronco
5	Campus is gorgeous
6	Fall quarter doesn't start until the end of September
7	Easy-going social scene
8	Intramural sports
9	Free wireless Internet network
10	Day parties

The Ten WORST Things About SCU

1	Tuition is expensive
2	Housing is expensive
3	Breathing is expensive
4	No nightclubs
5	No football
6	Spring quarter doesn't end until mid-June
7	Being hassled by Campus Safety
8	El Camino Real
9	Tyrannical meter maids
10	Small classes—you have to go all the time

Visiting

The Lowdown On...
Visiting

Hotel Information:

Best Western Airport Plaza
2118 The Alameda
San Jose, CA
(408) 243-2400
(800) 228-5150
Fax: (408) 243-5478
www.svhotels.com
Distance from Campus:
0.6 miles
Price: $65–$79

Biltmore Hotel & Suites
2151 Laurelwood Rd.
Santa Clara, CA
(408) 988-8411
(800) 255-9925
Fax: (408) 988-0225
www.hotelbiltmore.com
Distance from Campus:
4 miles
Price: $68–$134

→

Candlewood Suites

481 El Camino Real
Santa Clara, CA

(408) 241-9305

(888) 226-3539

Fax: (408) 241-9307

www.candlewoodsuites.com

Distance from Campus:
Less than 1 mile

Price: $105–$150

Courtyard by Marriott

1727 Technology Dr.
San Jose, CA

(408) 441-6111

(800) 321-2211

Fax: (408) 441-8039

www.courtyard.com

Distance from Campus:
3 miles

Price: $79–$229

Crowne Plaza

282 Almaden Blvd.
San Jose, CA

(408) 998-0400

Fax: (408) 279-1076

www.crowneplaza.com

Distance from Campus:
3 miles

Price: $99–$129

Days Inn

859 El Camino Real
Santa Clara, CA

(408) 244-2840

Fax: (408) 984-5720

www.daysinn.com

Distance from Campus:
Less than 1 mile

Price: $69–$89

Doubletree Hotel

2050 Gateway Pl.
San Jose, CA

(408) 453-4000

(800) 222-8733

Fax: (408) 437-2898

www.dtsj.com

Distance from Campus:
4 miles

Price: $109–$149

Embassy Suites Hotel

2885 Lakeside Dr.
Santa Clara, CA

(408) 496-6400

(800) 362-2779

Fax: (408) 988-7529

www.embassysuites.com

Distance from Campus:
4 miles

Price: $103–$149

Fairmont Hotel

170 S Market St.
San Jose, CA
(408) 998-1900
(800) 527-4727
Fax: (408) 287-1648
www.fairmont.com
Distance from Campus:
3 miles
Price: $239–$319

Hawthorn Suites

2455 El Camino Real
Santa Clara, CA
(408) 241-6444
(888) 770-8770
Fax: (408) 615-0286
www.svhotels.com
Distance from Campus:
2 miles
Price: $129–$149

Hilton – San Jose

300 Almaden Blvd.
San Jose, CA
(408) 287-2100
(800) HILTONS
Fax: (408) 947-4488
www.sanjose.hilton.com
Distance from Campus:
3 miles
Price: $129–$174

Hilton – Santa Clara

4949 Great America Pkwy.
Santa Clara, CA
(408) 330-0001
(800) HILTONS
Fax: (408) 330-0011
www.hiltonsantaclara.com
Distance from Campus:
6 miles
Price: $99–$154

Holiday Inn – Great America

4200 Great America Pkwy.
Santa Clara, CA
(408) 235-8900
(800) HOLIDAY
Fax: (408) 988-0976
www.holiday-inn.com
Distance from Campus:
4 miles
Price: $69–$105

Holiday Inn Express

1700 El Camino Real
Santa Clara, CA
(408) 554-9200
(800) 465-4329
Fax: (408) 554-8917
www.hiexpress.com
Distance from Campus:
3 miles
Price: $80–$119

Hotel De Anza

233 W Santa Clara St.
San Jose, CA

(408) 286-1000

(800) 843-3700

Fax: (408) 286-0500

www.hoteldeanza.com

Distance from Campus:
3 miles

Price: $109–$229

Howard Johnson Hotel

2499 El Camino Real
Santa Clara, CA

(408) 244-9610

Fax: 408 244-9541

*www.the.hojo.com/
santaclara02585*

Distance from Campus:
3 miles

Price: $55–$64

Hyatt – San Jose

1740 N First St.
San Jose, CA

(408) 793-3976

(888) 975-1234

Fax: (408) 453-0261

http://hyattsanjose.hyatt.com

Distance from Campus:
4 miles

Price: $79–$109

Hyatt – Santa Clara

5101 Great America Pkwy.
Santa Clara, CA

(408) 986-0700

Fax: (408) 980-3939

Distance from Campus:
6 miles

Price: $119–$139

Madison Street B&B Inn

1390 Madison St.
Santa Clara, CA

(408) 249-5541

(800) 791-5541

Fax: (408) 249-6676

www.madisonstreetinn.com

Distance from Campus:
1 mile

Price: $80–$150

Mariani's Inn

2500 El Camino Real
Santa Clara, CA

(408) 243-1431

(800) 553-8666

Fax: (408) 243-5745

www.marianis.com

Distance from Campus:
2 miles

Price: $79–$119

Marriott – Santa Clara

2700 Mission College Blvd.
Santa Clara, CA

(408) 988-1500

(800) 228-9290

Fax: (408) 727-4353

www.marriott.com

Distance from Campus:
5 miles

Price: $104–$229

The Plaza Suites

3100 Lakeside Dr.
Santa Clara, CA

(408) 748-9800

(800) 345-1554

Fax: (408) 986-1417

www.theplazasuites.com

Distance from Campus:
4 miles

Price: $129–$144

Radisson

1085 E El Camino Real
Sunnyvale, CA

(408) 247-0800

(800) 333-3333

Fax: (408) 984-7120

www.radisson.com

Distance from Campus:
2 miles

Price: $69–$219

Radisson Plaza Hotel

1471 N 4th St.
San Jose, CA

(408) 452-0200 x400

(800) 333-3333

Fax: (408) 457-8819

www.radisson.com

Distance from Campus:
5 miles

Price: $89–109

Toll House Hotel

140 S Santa Cruz
Los Gatos, CA

(408) 395-7070

(800) 238-6111

Fax: (408) 395-3730

www.tollhousehotel.com

Distance from Campus:
15 miles

Price: $160–$319

Vagabond Inn

3580 El Camino Real
Santa Clara, CA

(408) 241-0771

(800) 522-1555

Fax: (408) 247-3386

www.vagabondinns.com

Distance from Campus:
4 miles

Price: $50–$65

Wyndham Hotel

1350 N 1st St.
San Jose, CA

(408) 453-6200

(877) 999-3223

Fax: 408-437-9693

www.wyndham.com

Distance from Campus:
3 miles

Price: $75–$99

To Schedule a Group Information Session or Interview

Call (408) 554-4000 weekdays from 8 a.m.–5 p.m. PST.

Campus Tours

Campus tours run most Mondays through Fridays, September 27th to December 10th. Information sessions begin at 9:30 a.m. and 1:30 p.m., followed by tours at 10:30 a.m. and 2:30 p.m.

Directions to Campus

If you are coming from US Highway 101

• Take the De La Cruz Boulevard/Santa Clara exit.

• Follow De La Cruz Boulevard towards El Camino Real (stay in the right lane).

• When De La Cruz Boulevard splits, follow the right split over the overpass.

• Turn right on Lafayette Street staying in the right turn lane.

• Turn right at El Camino Real.

• The main entrance to Santa Clara University will be on the right side of the road.

If you are coming from Interstate 880

• Take the Alameda exit.

• Travel north on the Alameda.

• The Alameda will become El Camino Real.

• The main entrance to Santa Clara University will be on the left side of the road.

If you are coming from Interstate 280

• Take Interstate 880 North toward Oakland.

• Exit at the Alameda.

• Turn left on the Alameda.

• The Alameda will become El Camino Real.

• The main entrance to Santa Clara University will be on the left side of the road.

Words to Know

Academic Probation – A suspension imposed on a student if he or she fails to keep up with the school's minimum academic requirements. Those unable to improve their grades after receiving this warning can face dismissal.

Beer Pong/Beirut – A drinking game involving cups of beer arranged in a pyramid shape on each side of a table. The goal is to get a ping pong ball into one of the opponent's cups by throwing the ball or hitting it with a paddle. If the ball lands in a cup, the opponent is required to drink the beer.

Bid – An invitation from a fraternity or sorority to 'pledge' (join) that specific house.

Blue-Light Phone – Brightly-colored phone posts with a blue light bulb on top. These phones exist for security purposes and are located at various outside locations around most campuses. In an emergency, a student can pick up one of these phones (free of charge) to connect with campus police or a security escort.

Campus Police – Police who are specifically assigned to a given institution. Campus police are typically not regular city officers; they are employed by the university in a full-time capacity.

Club Sports – A level of sports that falls somewhere between varsity and intramural. If a student is unable to commit to a varsity team but has a lot of passion for athletics, a club sport could be a better, less intense option. Even less demanding, intramural (IM) sports often involve no traveling and considerably less time.

Cocaine – An illegal drug. Also known as "coke" or "blow," cocaine often resembles a white crystalline or powdery substance. It is highly addictive and dangerous.

Common Application – An application with which students can apply to multiple schools.

Course Registration – The period of official class selection for the upcoming quarter or semester. Prior to registration, it is best to prepare several back-up courses in case a particular class becomes full. If a course is full, students can place themselves on the waitlist, although this still does not guarantee entry.

Division Athletics – Athletic classifications range from Division I to Division III. Division IA is the most competitive, while Division III is considered to be the least competitive.

Dorm – A dorm (or dormitory) is an on-campus housing facility. Dorms can provide a range of options from suite-style rooms to more communal options that include shared bathrooms. Most first-year students live in dorms. Some upperclassmen who wish to stay on campus also choose this option.

Early Action – An application option with which a student can apply to a school and receive an early acceptance response without a binding commitment. This system is becoming less and less available.

Early Decision – An application option that students should use only if they are certain they plan to attend the school in question. If a student applies using the early decision option and is admitted, he or she is required and bound to attend that university. Admission rates are usually higher among students who apply through early decision, as the student is clearly indicating that the school is his or her first choice.

Ecstasy – An illegal drug. Also known as "E" or "X," ecstasy looks like a pill and most resembles an aspirin. Considered a party drug, ecstasy is very dangerous and can be deadly.

Ethernet – An extremely fast Internet connection available in most university-owned residence halls. To use an Ethernet connection properly, a student will need a network card and cable for his or her computer.

Fake ID – A counterfeit identification card that contains false information. Most commonly, students get fake IDs with altered birthdates so that they appear to be older than 21 (and therefore of legal drinking age). Even though it is illegal, many college students have fake IDs in hopes of purchasing alcohol or getting into bars.

Frosh – Slang for "freshman" or "freshmen."

Hazing – Initiation rituals administered by some fraternities or sororities as part of the pledging process. Many universities have outlawed hazing due to its degrading, and sometimes dangerous, nature.

Intramurals (IMs) – A popular, and usually free, sport league in which students create teams and compete against one another. These sports vary in competitiveness and can include a range of activities—everything from billiards to water polo. IM sports are a great way to meet people with similar interests.

Keg – Officially called a half-barrel, a keg contains roughly 200 12-ounce servings of beer.

LSD – An illegal drug, also known as acid, this hallucinogenic drug most commonly resembles a tab of paper.

Marijuana – An illegal drug, also known as weed or pot; along with alcohol, marijuana is one of the most commonly-found drugs on campuses across the country.

Major –The focal point of a student's college studies; a specific topic that is studied for a degree. Examples of majors include physics, English, history, computer science, economics, business, and music. Many students decide on a specific major before arriving on campus, while others are simply "undecided" until declaring a major. Those who are extremely interested in two areas can also choose to double major.

Meal Block – The equivalent of one meal. Students on a meal plan usually receive a fixed number of meals per week. Each meal, or "block," can be redeemed at the school's dining facilities in place of cash. Often, a student's weekly allotment of meal blocks will be forfeited if not used.

Minor – An additional focal point in a student's education. Often serving as a complement or addition to a student's main area of focus, a minor has fewer requirements and prerequisites to fulfill than a major. Minors are not required for graduation from most schools; however some students who want to explore many different interests choose to pursue both a major and a minor.

Mushrooms – An illegal drug. Also known as "'shrooms," this drug resembles regular mushrooms but is extremely hallucinogenic.

Off-Campus Housing – Housing from a particular landlord or rental group that is not affiliated with the university. Depending on the college, off-campus housing can range from extremely popular to non-existent. Students who choose to live off campus are typically given more freedom, but they also have to deal with possible subletting scenarios, furniture, bills, and other issues. In addition to these factors, rental prices and distance often affect a student's decision to move off campus.

Office Hours – Time that teachers set aside for students who have questions about coursework. Office hours are a good forum for students to go over any problems and to show interest in the subject material.

Pledging – The early phase of joining a fraternity or sorority, pledging takes place after a student has gone through rush and received a bid. Pledging usually lasts between one and two semesters. Once the pledging period is complete and a particular student has done everything that is required to become a member, that student is considered a brother or sister. If a fraternity or a sorority would decide to "haze" a group of students, this initiation would take place during the pledging period.

Private Institution – A school that does not use tax revenue to subsidize education costs. Private schools typically cost more than public schools and are usually smaller.

Prof – Slang for "professor."

Public Institution – A school that uses tax revenue to subsidize education costs. Public schools are often a good value for in-state residents and tend to be larger than most private colleges.

Quarter System (or Trimester System) – A type of academic calendar system. In this setup, students take classes for three academic periods. The first quarter usually starts in late September or early October and concludes right before Christmas. The second quarter usually starts around early to mid–January and finishes up around March or April. The last academic quarter, or "third quarter," usually starts in late March or early April and finishes up in late May or Mid-June. The fourth quarter is summer. The major difference between the quarter system and semester system is that students take more, less comprehensive courses under the quarter calendar.

RA (Resident Assistant) – A student leader who is assigned to a particular floor in a dormitory in order to help to the other students who live there. An RA's duties include ensuring student safety and providing assistance wherever possible.

Recitation – An extension of a specific course; a review session. Some classes, particularly large lectures, are supplemented with mandatory recitation sessions that provide a relatively personal class setting.

Rolling Admissions – A form of admissions. Most commonly found at public institutions, schools with this type of policy continue to accept students throughout the year until their class sizes are met. For example, some schools begin accepting students as early as December and will continue to do so until April or May.

Room and Board – This figure is typically the combined cost of a university-owned room and a meal plan.

Room Draw/Housing Lottery – A common way to pick on-campus room assignments for the following year. If a student decides to remain in university-owned housing, he or she is assigned a unique number that, along with seniority, is used to determine his or her housing for the next year.

Rush – The period in which students can meet the brothers and sisters of a particular chapter and find out if a given fraternity or sorority is right for them. Rushing a fraternity or a sorority is not a requirement at any school. The goal of rush is to give students who are serious about pledging a feel for what to expect.

Semester System – The most common type of academic calendar system at college campuses. This setup typically includes two semesters in a given school year. The fall semester starts around the end of August or early September and concludes before winter vacation. The spring semester usually starts in mid-January and ends in late April or May.

Student Center/Rec Center/Student Union – A common area on campus that often contains study areas, recreation facilities, and eateries. This building is often a good place to meet up with fellow students; depending on the school, the student center can have a huge role or a non-existent role in campus life.

Student ID – A university-issued photo ID that serves as a student's key to school-related functions. Some schools require students to show these cards in order to get into dorms, libraries, cafeterias, and other facilities. In addition to storing meal plan information, in some cases, a student ID can actually work as a debit card and allow students to purchase things from bookstores or local shops.

Suite – A type of dorm room. Unlike dorms that feature communal bathrooms shared by the entire floor, suites offer bathrooms shared only among the suite. Suite-style dorm rooms can house anywhere from two to ten students.

TA (Teacher's Assistant) – An undergraduate or grad student who helps in some manner with a specific course. In some cases, a TA will teach a class, assist a professor, grade assignments, or conduct office hours.

Undergraduate – A student in the process of studying for his or her bachelor's degree.

ABOUT THE AUTHOR

Al Schwartz is an English major at Santa Clara University. A native of Kansas, Al is an Aquarius, and was happy to do this book because it qualifies as a freelance writing assignment, and he thinks telling people he does "freelance" work sounds cool.

alschwartz@collegeprowler.com

Notes

....

....

....

....

....

....

....

....

....

....

....

....

....

Notes

....

....

....

....

....

....

....

....

....

....

....

....

....

Notes

....

....

....

....

....

....

....

....

....

....

....

....

....

Notes

....
....
....
....
....
....
....
....
....
....
....
....
....

Notes

....

....

....

....

....

....

....

....

....

....

....

....

....

Notes

....

....

....

....

....

....

....

....

....

....

....

....

....

Notes

....

....

....

....

....

....

....

....

....

....

....

....

....

Notes

....

....

....

....

....

....

....

....

....

....

....

....

....

Notes

....

....

....

....

....

....

....

....

....

....

....

....

....

Notes

....

....

....

....

....

....

....

....

....

....

....

....

....

Notes

....

....

....

....

....

....

....

....

....

....

....

....

....

Notes

....

....

....

....

....

....

....

....

....

....

....

....

....

Notes

....

....

....

....

....

....

....

....

....

....

....

....

....

Notes

....

....

....

....

....

....

....

....

....

....

....

....

....

Notes

....

....

....

....

....

....

....

....

....

....

....

....

....

....

Notes

....

....

....

....

....

....

....

....

....

....

....

....

....

Notes

....

....

....

....

....

....

....

....

....

....

....

....

....

Notes

....

....

....

....

....

....

....

....

....

....

....

....

....

Notes

....

....

....

....

....

....

....

....

....

....

....

....

....

Notes

....

....

....

....

....

....

....

....

....

....

....

....

....

Notes

....

....

....

....

....

....

....

....

....

....

....

....

....

Notes

....

....

....

....

....

....

....

....

....

....

....

....

....

Notes

....

....

....

....

....

....

....

....

....

....

....

....

....

....

Notes

....

....

....

....

....

....

....

....

....

....

....

....

....

....

Notes

....

....

....

....

....

....

....

....

....

....

....

....

....

....

Notes

....

....

....

....

....

....

....

....

....

....

....

....

....

Notes

....

....

....

....

....

....

....

....

....

....

....

....

....

Notes

....

....

....

....

....

....

....

....

....

....

....

....

....

Notes

....

....

....

....

....

....

....

....

....

....

....

....

....

Notes

....

....

....

....

....

....

....

....

....

....

....

....

....

Notes

....

....

....

....

....

....

....

....

....

....

....

....

....

Notes

....

....

....

....

....

....

....

....

....

....

....

....

....

Notes

....

....

....

....

....

....

....

....

....

....

....

....

....

California Colleges

California dreamin'?
This book is a must have for you!

CALIFORNIA COLLEGES
7¼" X 10", 762 Pages Paperback
$29.95 Retail
1-59658-501-3

Stanford, UC Berkeley, Caltech—California is home to some of America's greatest institutes of higher learning. *California Colleges* gives the lowdown on 24 of the best, side by side, in one prodigious volume.

New England College

Looking for peace in the Northeast?
Pick up this regional guide to New England!

NEW ENGLAND COLLEGES
7¼" X 10", 1015 Pages Paperback
$29.95 Retail
1-59658-504-8

New England is the birthplace of many prestigious universities, and with so many to choose from, picking the right school can be a tough decision. With inside information on over 34 competive Northeastern schools, *New England Colleges* provides the same high-quality information prospective students expect from College Prowler in one all-inclusive, easy-to-use reference.

Schools of the South

Headin' down south? This book will help you find your way to the perfect school!

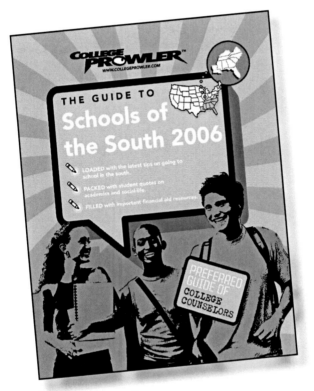

SCHOOLS OF THE SOUTH
7¼" X 10", 773 Pages Paperback
$29.95 Retail
1-59658-503-X

Southern pride is always strong. Whether it's across town or across state, many Southern students are devoted to their home sweet home. *Schools of the South* offers an honest student perspective on 36 universities available south of the Mason-Dixon.

Untangling
the Ivy League

The ultimate book for everything Ivy!

UNTANGLING THE IVY LEAGUE
7¼" X 10", 567 Pages Paperback
$24.95 Retail
1-59658-500-5

Ivy League students, alumni, admissions officers,
and other top insiders get together to tell it like it is.
Untangling the Ivy League covers every aspect—from
admissions and athletics to secret societies and urban
legends—of the nation's eight oldest, wealthiest, and
most competitive colleges and universities.

Tell Us What Life Is Really Like at Your School!

Have you ever wanted to let people know what your college is really like? Now's your chance to help millions of high school students choose the right college.

Let your voice be heard.

Check out **www.collegeprowler.com** for more info!

Need More Help?

Do you have more questions about this school? Can't find a certain statistic? College Prowler is here to help. We are the best source of college information out there. We have a network of thousands of students who can get the latest information on any school to you ASAP. E-mail us at info@collegeprowler.com with your college-related questions.

E-Mail Us Your College-Related Questions!

Check out *www.collegeprowler.com* for more details.
1-800-290-2682

Write For Us!
Get published! Voice your opinion.

Writing a College Prowler guidebook is both fun and
rewarding; our open-ended format allows your own
creativity free reign. Our writers have been featured
in national newspapers and have seen their names in
bookstores across the country. Now is your chance
to break into the publishing industry with one of the
country's fastest-growing publishers!

Apply now at *www.collegeprowler.com*

Contact editor@collegeprowler.com or
call 1-800-290-2682 for more details.

Pros and Cons

Still can't figure out if this is the right school for you?
You've already read through this in-depth guide; why not
list the pros and cons? It will really help with narrowing down
your decision and determining whether or not
this school is right for you.

Pros	Cons
....	....
....	....
....	....
....	....
....	....
....	....
....	....
....	....
....	....
....	....
....	....
....	....
....	....

Pros and Cons

Still can't figure out if this is the right school for you?
You've already read through this in-depth guide; why not
list the pros and cons? It will really help with narrowing down
your decision and determining whether or not
this school is right for you.

Pros	Cons
....	....
....	....
....	....
....	....
....	....
....	....
....	....
....	....
....	....
....	....
....	....
....	....
....	....

Notes

....

....

....

....

....

....

....

....

....

....

....

....

....

Notes

....

....

....

....

....

....

....

....

....

....

....

....

....